DONUTS

50
sticky-hot donut
recipes to make
at home

Tracey Meharg

D0824731

8/19 ⑦ ᴜᴅ 9/18

DONUTS

50 sticky-hot donut recipes to make at home

Tracey Meharg

STERLING EPICURE
New York

CONTENTS

The **donut** through **time**

Have you ever eaten a donut fresh out of the fryer or straight from the oven? If you have, you know how huge the gulf is between them and those stale off-the-shelf donuts, with their faux-cream, waxy frosting and gooey fillings. Making your own is a commitment, but if you know how a good donut tastes, you'll know that these hot, scrumptious morsels are worth the effort. Recently, the real thing — the donut as it was meant to be — has been finding its way into more and more high-end restaurants and bakeries, with the food industry catching on that the donut, done right, can be truly sensational.

Donuts as we know them were brought over from the Netherlands to Manhattan in the early 1800s, when this area was still known as New Amsterdam. Called *olykoeks* or *oliebollen* — literally "oil-cakes" or "oil-balls" — they were filled with dried fruit and spices before being fried in oil, and are still a Christmas favorite in the Netherlands.

They were revolutionized in the 1840s when a ship-captain's mother, Elizabeth Gregory, cooked them for the crew — she put walnuts and hazelnuts in the middle (hence "doughnuts"), perhaps to make them healthier, or perhaps to keep them from being so greasy in the middle. Her son Hanson is credited with inventing the donut hole by cutting it out of the dough with a small can, thereby transforming the donut into something that could be fried evenly all the way around. (Or, as another version of the story goes, he was at the ship's wheel when a storm hit, and he had to quickly impale the donut he was eating on a spoke so he could use both hands to steady the ship, accidentally making culinary history!)

After tin donut cutters were patented in 1867, donuts fast became a staple in American homes, and by World War I they were so iconic that volunteers gave them out in the trenches in France to remind the soldiers of home. Soon after that came Joseph Levitt's infamous donut machine, which became a public spectacle in New York: the circle of dough dropping off into the vat of boiling oil, circulating, and then turning over, browning and emerging on a motorized ramp. It was a futuristic mystery, a sensation that had to be experienced first-hand.

But what is it about donuts that makes them so damn delicious? The secret is the temperature of the oil they are cooked in — by dropping them in very hot oil, the superheated steam puffs them up with air, making them literally light and fluffy. That, along with the hole, means the donut gets super hot, super fast: never doughy or dense.

The same goes for oven-baked donuts, which are just as delicious. They get hot fast, and that classic hole in the middle ensures they cook evenly, crisping up on the outside but staying fresh and steamy on the inside.

There are other iconic donuts across the world too, of course: the Israeli Hannukah specialty *sufganiyot* is now known worldwide as the godfather of the jam or jelly donut. There's also the slightly saltier, chocolate-dipped Mexican *churro*, which has its own mysterious origins: it may have been brought over by the Portuguese via China, or was possibly invented by Spanish shepherds as an alternative bread that could be cooked in the open air. Or from France, there's the *Pets de Nonne*, or nun's farts, a crispy-tender dough, often thickly dusted in powdered sugar. There's also more than a few Eastern takes on the donut, including the Indian *jalebi*, a celebration sweet which is a kind of pretzel-shaped donut, deep-fried and dipped in sugar syrup.

Now almost every country has their own homespun version, be they cream or custard-filled, topped with candy for the kids or made with healthy options that combine the donut's perfect anatomy with whole foods and natural sugars.

Somewhere along the way, though, as it journeyed across the world, did the donut lose its zap? It made its way into hearts worldwide as a fast, delicious, tongue-burning treat, but has over the years become doughier, staler, neglected, made to sit on shelves for too long. But it doesn't have to be like that: it should be eaten fresh, and can be delectable fried or baked. It isn't doomed to die a death by preservatives and icing!

Donuts came from the home at Christmas-time, when it was coldest, and became so well-loved because they're heart-warming, decadent and comforting. Now they're back on gourmet menus, along with the introduction of the unlikely but undeniably fabulous croissant-donut. You don't need a deep-fryer to get these right, and they don't have to be greasy or doughy: they can be airy, fluffy and heavenly. So roll up your sleeves, and get them while they're hot!

CHAPTER 1

BASICS

YEAST DONUTS

These donuts have a lovely soft and chewy texture, making it hard to stop at just one. For the best results, be sure to enjoy these the same day you make them.

YEAST DONUTS

1 cup lukewarm milk
3½ teaspoons dried yeast
3⅔ cups all-purpose flour, plus extra for dusting
¼ cup superfine sugar
A good pinch of fine sea salt
1 egg, at room temperature, lightly whisked
2 tablespoons unsalted butter, melted, at room temperature

WHISK the milk and yeast together in a small bowl. Add 1 teaspoon of the flour and 1 teaspoon of the sugar, then whisk until well combined. Allow to stand at room temperature in a warm spot for 10–15 minutes, or until frothy.

PLACE the remaining flour, remaining sugar, and the salt in the bowl of a stand mixer. Attach the dough hook and mix together on medium speed until well combined.

WITH the motor running, slowly add the egg, melted butter, and the yeast mixture. Mix for 8 minutes, or until the dough is smooth and elastic (the dough should feel slightly sticky).

USING very lightly floured hands, scrape the dough into a lightly oiled bowl. Cover with a piece of parchment paper, then a dish towel. Set aside to rest in a warm, draft-free spot and leave for 1–1½ hours, or until the dough has doubled in size. (See pages 14–17, Tips for making yeast donuts.)

LINE two large baking trays with parchment paper. Generously flour a work surface and gently tip the dough out onto it. Using a floured rolling pin, gently roll the dough out to a ⅓ inch thickness. Using a floured 3½ inch round cookie cutter, cut out 10 rounds from the dough, making sure you cut them as close together as possible. Use a floured 1⅛ inch round cookie cutter to cut out holes from the center of each larger circle. Carefully transfer the donuts and their holes to the prepared trays, spreading them out in a single layer. Cover with dish towels then allow to rest for 40 minutes at room temperature, or until the donuts have doubled in size.

DEEP-FRY or bake and coat in cinnamon sugar as instructed on pages 30–31. Serve hot, warm, or at room temperature.

Tips for making
yeast donuts

The dough needs to be left for 1–1½ hours to rise.

Use a floured rolling pin to gently roll out the dough.

Cut out rounds from the dough, making sure you cut them as close together as possible.

Cut out holes from the center of each larger circle.

CAKE DONUTS

These donuts are wonderfully quick to make — just like whipping up a cake batter — and are sure to be a hit with the kids, too. Enjoy them on the day you make them, or store overnight in an airtight container at room temperature and reheat for a few seconds in the microwave until warm.

CAKE DONUTS

5 tablespoons + 2 teaspoons
   unsalted butter, at room
   temperature
½ cup superfine sugar
1 egg, at room temperature
1 egg yolk, at room temperature
1 teaspoon vanilla extract
¾ cup milk
4 cups self-rising flour,
   plus extra for dusting
A good pinch of fine sea salt

CREAM the butter and sugar together in the bowl of a stand mixer for 3 minutes, or until pale and fluffy. Add the egg, egg yolk, vanilla extract, and milk and mix until just combined.

SIFT the flour and salt over the mixture in the bowl. Mix until just combined, but do not overmix or the dough will become tough. (See pages 20–23, Tips for making cake donuts.)

LIGHTLY flour a work surface, turn the dough out onto it and, using lightly floured hands, gently bring together. Knead gently for a few seconds until the dough becomes smooth. Using a floured rolling pin, gently roll the dough out to a ⅓ inch thickness. Using a floured 3½ inch round cookie cutter, cut out rounds from the dough, making sure you cut them as close together as possible. Re-roll any scraps and cut out more rounds until you have 12 in total. Use a floured 1⅛ inch round cookie cutter to cut out holes from the center of each larger circle.

DEEP-FRY or bake and coat in cinnamon sugar as instructed on pages 30–31. Serve hot, warm, or at room temperature.

Tips for making
cake donuts

Mix the dough until just combined — do not overmix or the donuts will be tough.

Bring the dough together with your hands and knead gently.

Use a floured rolling pin to gently roll out the dough.

CROISSANT-DONUTS

A wonderfully decadent combination: croissant meets donut. A little patience and time is all that's needed to prepare these, and they are well worth the effort.

CROISSANT-DONUTS
¾ cup lukewarm milk
3 teaspoons dried yeast
¼ cup superfine sugar
2 eggs, at room temperature, lightly whisked
1 teaspoon vanilla extract
3⅔ cups all-purpose flour, plus extra for dusting
A good pinch of fine sea salt

BUTTER MIXTURE
¼ cup all-purpose flour
14 tablespoons unsalted butter, at room temperature

COMBINE the milk, yeast, sugar, eggs, vanilla extract, flour, and salt in the bowl of a stand mixer. Attach the dough hook then mix on low speed until the ingredients are well combined. Increase the speed to medium–low and mix for 4 minutes, or until the dough is smooth and elastic (the dough will be sticky).

LINE a baking tray with parchment paper that's been lightly floured, then transfer the dough. Using lightly floured fingertips, flatten the dough into a rectangle shape roughly 8 x 6 inches. Cover with a piece of parchment paper and refrigerate for 30 minutes.

BEAT the flour and butter for the butter mixture in the bowl of a stand mixer until smooth. Remove the chilled dough from the fridge and transfer it on the parchment paper to a work surface. With a lightly floured rolling pin, roll out the dough to a ¼ inch thick rectangle roughly 12 x 8 inches. Spread the butter mixture evenly over the dough, making sure you spread it right to the edges. (See pages 26–9, Tips for making croissant-donuts.)

FOLD the dough in thirds from the shorter sides, like a letter, then transfer back onto the tray on the parchment paper. Cover with another sheet of parchment paper and refrigerate for 30 minutes.

REMOVE the dough from the fridge and transfer to a clean piece of parchment paper lightly dusted with flour. Turn the dough 90 degrees and roll it into the same-sized rectangle again, then fold both edges to the middle. Refrigerate for another 30 minutes, then repeat the whole turning, rolling, folding, and chilling sequence twice more. Finally, turn, roll, and fold the dough, then chill it for 1 hour.

LINE a large baking tray with parchment paper. Lightly flour a work surface and a rolling pin and roll the chilled dough out to a ¼ inch thick rectangle roughly 12 x 8 inches. Using a floured 3½ inch round cookie cutter, cut out eight rounds from the dough, making sure you cut them as close together as possible. Use a floured 1⅛ inch round cookie cutter to cut out holes from the center of each larger circle. Carefully transfer the croissant-donuts and their holes to a prepared tray in a single layer. Cover with a dish towel. Set aside to rest for 40 minutes at room temperature, or until they have doubled in size.

DEEP-FRY and coat in cinnamon sugar as instructed on pages 30–31. Serve hot, warm, or at room temperature.

Tips for making
croissant-donuts

Spread the butter mixture evenly over the rolled-out dough, right to the edges.

Roll out the dough with a lightly floured rolling pin.

Fold the dough into thirds, like a letter.

How to **deep-fry**

When deep-frying donuts, make sure you use a saucepan that allows for a minimum depth of 2 inches for the oil. Only add the donuts to the oil when it has reached the desired temperature, otherwise they'll absorb too much oil and become heavy, rather than light and fluffy. To check this, you'll need a sugar thermometer, or you can drop a small amount of dough into the heated oil: it will immediately bubble around the edges if the oil is hot enough.

Vegetable, canola, or rice bran oil, for deep-frying

HEAT the oil in a deep-fryer or a deep, heavy-based saucepan over medium–high heat, or until the oil temperature reaches 350°F.

DEEP-FRY the donuts in batches, turning occasionally, for 2–3 minutes each, until puffed, golden, and cooked through. Transfer to paper towels to drain before coating (see opposite) and serving.

DEEP-FRY the donut holes in three separate batches for 1–2 minutes each, or until puffed, golden, and cooked through. Transfer to paper towels to drain before coating (see opposite) and serving.

How to **bake**

Baking donuts is a healthy alternative to deep-frying. You may find that some of the holes in the donuts close slightly on baking — if that happens, simply use the end of a wooden spoon to gently re-open the holes while the donuts are still hot.

½ cup unsalted butter, melted

PREHEAT the oven to 350°F. Line two large baking trays with parchment paper. Place the donuts and donut holes 1⅛ inches apart on the prepared trays.

BAKE the donuts, one tray at a time, for 10–12 minutes, or until puffed, light golden, and cooked through (the donuts will sound hollow when their bases are tapped). Allow to cool for 3 minutes on the tray.

BRUSH lightly all over with the melted butter before coating (see below) and serving.

TO COAT
Everyone's favorite topping for donuts is cinnamon sugar. For 8–12 donuts, you'll need 1 cup sugar — granulated sugar is best — and 2 teaspoons ground cinnamon. Combine the sugar and cinnamon in a deep, heatproof bowl for coating the donuts.

Muesli donuts

Espresso cream-filled donuts

Lemon and poppy seed donuts

Maple syrup-glazed donuts
with crispy prosciutto

Blueberry donuts
with Earl Grey glaze

Peanut butter and
strawberry jam donuts

Banana donuts

Pretzel donuts

CHAPTER

2

WAKE UP
AND SMELL THE
DONUTS

MUESLI DONUTS

The perfect grab-and-go breakfast treat — all you need is a paper napkin.

CAKE DONUTS

5 tablespoons + 2 teaspoons
   unsalted butter, at room
   temperature
½ cup firmly packed
   light brown sugar
1 egg, at room temperature
1 egg yolk, at room temperature
2 teaspoons vanilla bean paste
¾ cup milk
4 cups self-rising flour,
   plus extra for dusting
A good pinch of fine sea salt
Vegetable, canola, or rice bran
   oil, for deep-frying

YOGURT ICING

¼ cup Greek-style vanilla yogurt
1½ cups confectioners' sugar

TO SERVE

¾ cup store-bought toasted
   muesli with dried fruit

CREAM the butter and brown sugar together in the bowl of a stand mixer for 3 minutes, or until pale and fluffy. Add the egg, egg yolk, vanilla bean paste, and milk. Mix until just combined.

SIFT the flour and salt over the mixture in the bowl. Mix until just combined, but do not overmix or the dough will become tough.

LIGHTLY flour a clean surface, turn the dough out onto it and, using lightly floured hands, gently bring together. Knead gently for a few seconds until the dough becomes smooth. Using a floured rolling pin, gently roll the dough out to a ⅓ inch thickness. Using a floured 3½ inch round cookie cutter, cut out rounds from the dough, making sure you cut them as close together as possible. Re-roll any scraps of dough and cut out more rounds until you have 12 in total. Use a floured 1⅛ inch round cookie cutter to cut out holes from the center of each larger circle.

HEAT the oil in a deep, heavy-based saucepan over medium–high heat until it reaches 350°F. Deep-fry the donuts in batches, turning occasionally, for 2–3 minutes each, or until puffed, golden, and cooked through. Transfer to paper towels to drain, then allow to cool.

WHISK all of the ingredients for the yogurt icing together in a bowl until well combined and smooth.

SPREAD the icing over the donuts, then transfer to a wire rack set over a baking tray. Decorate the tops with toasted muesli and allow to set before serving.

ESPRESSO CREAM-FILLED DONUTS

These are guaranteed to boost a coffee-lover's energy levels in the morning!

YEAST DONUTS
1 cup lukewarm milk
3½ teaspoons dried yeast
3⅔ cups all-purpose flour,
    plus extra for dusting
¼ cup superfine sugar
A good pinch of fine sea salt
1 egg, at room temperature,
    lightly whisked
2 tablespoons unsalted butter,
    melted, at room temperature
Vegetable, canola, or rice bran
    oil, for deep-frying

TO COAT
1 cup sugar
2 teaspoons ground cinnamon

ESPRESSO CREAM
1¼ cups whipping cream
2 tablespoons espresso
    coffee, cooled
½ cup superfine sugar

WHISK the milk and yeast together in a small bowl. Add 1 teaspoon of the flour and 1 teaspoon of the sugar and whisk until well combined. Allow to stand in a warm spot for 10–15 minutes, or until frothy.

PLACE the remaining flour, remaining sugar, and the salt in the bowl of a stand mixer. Attach the dough hook and mix together on medium speed until well combined.

WITH the motor running, slowly add the egg, melted butter, and the yeast mixture. Mix for 8 minutes, or until the dough is smooth and elastic (the dough should feel slightly sticky).

USING very lightly floured hands, scrape the dough into a lightly oiled bowl. Cover with a piece of parchment paper then a dish towel. Set aside to rest at room temperature in a warm, draft-free spot for 1–1½ hours, or until the dough has doubled in size.

LINE two large baking trays with parchment paper. Generously flour a work surface and gently tip the dough out onto it. Using a floured rolling pin, gently roll the dough out to a ⅓ inch thickness. Using a floured 2⅓ inch round cookie cutter, cut out 18 rounds from the dough, making sure you cut them as close together as possible. Carefully transfer the donuts to the prepared trays, spreading them out in a single layer. Cover with dish towels and allow to rest for 40 minutes at room temperature, or until doubled in size.

COMBINE the sugar and cinnamon, for coating the donuts, in a deep, heatproof bowl.

HEAT the oil in a deep, heavy-based saucepan over medium–high heat until it reaches 350°F. Deep-fry the donuts in batches, turning occasionally, for 2–3 minutes each, or until puffed, golden, and cooked through. Transfer to paper towels to drain briefly and, while still hot, gently toss in the cinnamon sugar to coat on all sides. Allow to cool.

BEAT all the ingredients for the espresso cream together in a bowl until soft peaks form.

SPOON the mixture into a piping bag fitted with a ¼ inch round tip, then pipe into the center of each donut and serve.

LEMON AND POPPY SEED DONUTS

Pretty and delicious, these are a lovely take on muffins.

CAKE DONUTS

5 tablespoons + 2 teaspoons
  unsalted butter, at room
  temperature
½ cup superfine sugar
1 egg, at room temperature
1 egg yolk, at room temperature
1 teaspoon vanilla extract
¾ cup milk
4 cups self-rising flour,
  plus extra for dusting
A good pinch of fine sea salt
1 tablespoon poppy seeds
2 tablespoons finely grated
  lemon zest
Vegetable, canola, or rice bran
  oil, for deep-frying

TO COAT

1 cup sugar

LEMON BUTTERCREAM

¼ cup unsalted butter,
  at room temperature
2 cups confectioners' sugar
2 tablespoons lemon juice

TO SERVE

1 teaspoon poppy seeds
Lemon zest

CREAM the butter and sugar together in the bowl of a stand mixer for 3 minutes, or until pale and fluffy. Add the egg, egg yolk, vanilla extract, and milk and mix until just combined.

SIFT the flour and salt over the mixture in the bowl. Add the poppy seeds and the lemon zest. Mix until just combined, but do not overmix or the dough will become tough.

LIGHTLY flour a clean surface, turn the dough out onto it and, using lightly floured hands, gently bring together. Knead gently for a few seconds until the dough becomes smooth. Using a floured rolling pin, gently roll the dough out to a ⅓ inch thickness. Using a floured 3½ inch round cookie cutter, cut out rounds from the dough, making sure you cut them as close together as possible. Re-roll any scraps and cut out more rounds until you have 12 in total. Use a floured 1⅛ inch round cookie cutter to cut out holes from the center of each larger circle.

PLACE the sugar for coating in a deep, heatproof bowl.

HEAT the oil in a deep, heavy-based saucepan over medium–high heat until it reaches 350°F. Deep-fry the donuts in batches, turning occasionally, for 2–3 minutes each, or until puffed, golden, and cooked through. Transfer to paper towels to drain briefly and, while still hot, gently toss and roll in the sugar to coat on all sides. Allow to cool.

BEAT the butter for the buttercream for 3 minutes, or until very pale in color and fluffy. Add the remaining ingredients and beat until well combined and smooth.

SPOON the buttercream into a piping bag fitted with a ⅓ inch star tip then pipe it over the center of each donut. Sprinkle the tops with poppy seeds and lemon zest, then serve.

MAPLE SYRUP-GLAZED DONUTS WITH CRISPY PROSCIUTTO

The perfect balance of sweet and salty flavors, with the added crunch of crispy prosciutto.

YEAST DONUTS

1 cup lukewarm milk
3½ teaspoons dried yeast
3⅔ cups all-purpose flour,
    plus extra for dusting
¼ cup superfine sugar
A good pinch of fine sea salt
1 egg, at room temperature,
    lightly whisked
2 tablespoons unsalted butter,
    melted, at room temperature
Vegetable, canola, or rice bran
    oil, for deep-frying

TO SERVE

4 thin slices prosciutto

MAPLE SYRUP GLAZE

1 cup confectioners' sugar, sifted
⅓ cup maple syrup

WHISK the milk and yeast together in a small bowl. Add 1 teaspoon of the flour and 1 teaspoon of the sugar and whisk until well combined. Allow to stand in a warm spot for 10–15 minutes, or until frothy.

PLACE the remaining flour, remaining sugar, and the salt in the bowl of a stand mixer. Attach the dough hook and mix together on medium speed until well combined.

WITH the motor running, slowly add the egg, melted butter and the yeast mixture. Mix for 8 minutes, or until the dough is smooth and elastic (the dough should feel slightly sticky).

USING very lightly floured hands, scrape the dough into a lightly oiled bowl. Cover with a piece of parchment paper, then a dish towel. Set aside to rest in a warm, draft-free spot for 1–1½ hours, or until the dough has doubled in size.

LINE two large baking trays with parchment paper. Generously flour a work surface and gently tip the dough out onto it. Using a floured rolling pin, gently roll the dough out to a ⅓ inch thickness. Using a 3½ inch round cookie cutter, cut out 10 rounds from the dough, making sure you cut them as close together as possible. Use a floured 1⅛ inch round cookie cutter to cut out holes from the center of each donut. Carefully transfer the donuts to the prepared trays, spreading them out in a single layer. Cover with dish towels. Rest for 40 minutes at room temperature or until doubled in size.

HEAT the oil in a deep, heavy-based saucepan over medium–high heat until it reaches 350°F. Deep-fry the donuts in batches, turning occasionally, for 2–3 minutes each, or until puffed, golden, and cooked through. Transfer to paper towels to drain briefly. Allow to cool.

MEANWHILE, cook the prosciutto on a foil-lined baking tray under the broiler for 2–3 minutes, or until crisp and golden. Allow to cool, then break into small pieces.

WHISK the ingredients for the maple syrup glaze together in a bowl until well combined and smooth.

DIP the donuts, one at a time, into the glaze, then transfer to a wire rack set over a baking tray. Decorate the tops with prosciutto pieces and allow to set before serving.

BLUEBERRY DONUTS WITH EARL GREY GLAZE

The Earl Grey tea glaze on these donuts makes them a delicious addition to any morning tea.

CAKE DONUTS

5 tablespoons + 2 teaspoons
   unsalted butter, at room
   temperature
½ cup superfine sugar
1 egg, at room temperature
1 egg yolk, at room temperature
½ cup dried blueberries
1 teaspoon vanilla extract
¾ cup milk
4 cups self-rising flour,
   plus extra for dusting
A good pinch of fine sea salt
Vegetable, canola, or rice bran
   oil, for deep-frying
1⅔ cups blueberries

EARL GREY GLAZE

1 Earl Grey tea bag
¼ cup boiling water
1 cup confectioners' sugar

CREAM the butter and sugar together in the bowl of a stand mixer for 3 minutes, or until pale and fluffy. Add the egg, egg yolk, dried blueberries, vanilla extract, and milk and mix until just combined.

SIFT the flour and salt over the mixture in the bowl. Mix until just combined, but do not overmix or the dough will become tough.

LIGHTLY flour a clean surface, turn the dough out onto it and, using lightly floured hands, gently bring together. Knead gently for a few seconds until the dough becomes smooth. Using a floured rolling pin, gently roll the dough out to a ⅓ inch thickness. Using a floured 3½ inch round cookie cutter, cut out rounds from the dough, making sure you cut them as close together as possible. Re-roll any scraps and cut out more rounds until you have 12 in total. Use a floured 1⅛ inch round cookie cutter to cut out holes from the center of each larger circle.

HEAT the oil in a deep, heavy-based saucepan over medium–high heat until it reaches 350°F. Deep-fry the donuts in batches, turning occasionally, for 2–3 minutes each, or until puffed, golden, and cooked through. Transfer to paper towels to drain. Allow to cool.

TO make the glaze, steep the tea bag in the boiling water for 5 minutes. Remove and discard tea bag, then whisk the confectioners' sugar and tea together in a bowl until well combined and smooth.

DIP the donuts, one at a time, in the glaze, then transfer to a wire rack set over a baking tray. Decorate the tops with fresh blueberries and allow to set before serving.

TIP YOU CAN ALSO DECORATE THE DONUTS WITH SMALL EDIBLE FLOWERS SUCH AS LAVENDER OR DRIED ROSE PETALS, IF YOU LIKE.

PEANUT BUTTER AND STRAWBERRY JAM DONUTS

Lock up your donuts! The kids will go crazy for these sweet 'n' salty treats.

CAKE DONUTS

3½ tablespoons unsalted butter, at room temperature
½ cup crunchy peanut butter
½ cup superfine sugar
1 egg, at room temperature
1 egg yolk, at room temperature
½ teaspoon vanilla extract
¾ cup milk
4 cups self-rising flour, plus extra for dusting
Vegetable, canola, or rice bran oil, for deep-frying

TO COAT

1 cup sugar

TO SERVE

¾ cup strawberry jam, warmed
1½ cups small strawberries, thinly sliced

CREAM the butter, peanut butter, and sugar together in the bowl of a stand mixer for 3 minutes, or until pale and fluffy. Add the egg, egg yolk, vanilla extract, and milk and mix until just combined.

SIFT the flour over the mixture in the bowl. Mix until just combined, but do not overmix or the dough will become tough.

LIGHTLY flour a clean surface, turn the dough out onto it and, using lightly floured hands, gently bring together. Knead gently for a few seconds until the dough becomes smooth. Using a floured rolling pin, gently roll the dough out to a ⅓ inch thickness. Using a floured 3½ inch round cookie cutter, cut out rounds from the dough, making sure you cut them as close together as possible. Re-roll any scraps and cut out more rounds until you have 12 in total. Use a floured 1⅛ inch round cookie cutter to cut out holes from the center of each larger circle.

PLACE the sugar for coating in a deep, heatproof bowl.

HEAT the oil in a deep, heavy-based saucepan over medium–high heat until it reaches 350°F. Deep-fry the donuts in batches, turning occasionally, for 2–3 minutes each, or until puffed, golden, and cooked through. Transfer to paper towels to drain briefly, then gently roll the donuts in the sugar to coat the sides, and allow to cool.

SPOON the warm jam over the tops of the donuts and decorate with the strawberry slices. Allow to set before serving.

TIP YOU CAN ALSO DECORATE THE TOPS OF THE DONUT WITH CRUSHED, UNSALTED PEANUTS.

BANANA DONUTS

These heavenly donuts are baked, not fried, which means you can enjoy a few without feeling too guilty!

CAKE DONUTS

5 tablespoons + 2 teaspoons unsalted butter, at room temperature
½ cup firmly packed brown sugar
2 medium over-ripe bananas
1 egg, at room temperature
1 egg yolk, at room temperature
1 teaspoon vanilla extract
¾ cup milk
4⅓ cups self-rising flour
A good pinch of fine sea salt
¼ teaspoon ground cinnamon

CINNAMON GLAZE

1 cup confectioners' sugar
½ teaspoon ground cinnamon
1½ tablespoons water

TO TOP

½ cup coarsely chopped walnuts, toasted
2 tablespoons coconut chips, toasted
2 tablespoons roughly crushed banana chips

CREAM the butter and sugar together in the bowl of a stand mixer for 3 minutes, or until pale and fluffy. Add the bananas, egg, egg yolk, vanilla extract, and milk and mix until just combined.

SIFT the flour, salt, and cinnamon over the mixture in the bowl. Mix until just combined, but do not overmix or the dough will become tough.

LIGHTLY flour a clean surface, turn the dough out onto it and, using lightly floured hands, gently bring together. Knead gently for a few seconds until the dough becomes smooth. Using a floured rolling pin, gently roll the dough out to a ⅓ inch thickness. Using a floured 3½ inch round cookie cutter, cut out rounds from the dough, making sure you cut them as close together as possible. Re-roll any scraps and cut out more rounds until you have 12 in total. Use a floured 1⅛ inch round cookie cutter to cut out holes from the center of each larger circle.

PREHEAT the oven to 350°F. Line two large baking trays with parchment paper. Place the donuts about 1⅛ inches apart on the prepared trays.

BAKE each tray of donuts for 12–15 minutes, or until puffed, light golden, and cooked through (the donuts will sound hollow when the bases are tapped). Allow to cool on the trays for 3 minutes.

WHISK all of the cinnamon glaze ingredients together in a bowl until well combined and smooth.

DIP the donuts, one at a time, in the glaze, then transfer to a wire rack set over a baking tray. Sprinkle the tops with the walnuts, coconut chips, and banana chips. Allow to set before serving.

PRETZEL DONUTS

These won't last long straight from the pan, and are perfect served alongside coffee.

YEAST DONUTS
1 cup lukewarm milk
3½ teaspoons dried yeast
3 cups all-purpose flour, plus extra for dusting
¼ cup superfine sugar
½ cup mini salted pretzels, crushed
A good pinch of fine sea salt
1 egg, at room temperature, lightly whisked
5 tablespoons + 2 teaspoons unsalted butter, melted, at room temperature
Vegetable, canola, or rice bran oil, for deep-frying

TO COAT
1 cup sugar
2 teaspoons ground cinnamon

WHISK the milk and yeast together in a small bowl. Add 1 teaspoon of the flour and 1 teaspoon of the sugar and whisk until well combined. Allow to stand at room temperature in a warm spot for 10–15 minutes, or until frothy.

PLACE the remaining flour, remaining sugar, the crushed pretzels, and the salt in the bowl of a stand mixer. Attach the dough hook and mix together on medium speed until well combined.

WITH the motor running, slowly add the egg, melted butter, and the yeast mixture. Mix for 8 minutes, or until the dough is smooth and elastic (the dough should feel slightly sticky).

USING very lightly floured hands, scrape the dough into a lightly oiled bowl. Cover with a piece of parchment paper, then a dish towel. Set aside to rest at room temperature in a warm, draft-free spot for 1–1½ hours, or until the dough has doubled in size.

LINE two large baking trays with parchment paper. Generously flour a work surface and gently tip the dough out onto it. Using a floured rolling pin, gently roll the dough out to a ⅓ inch thick rectangle about 12 x 11 inches. Cut the rectangle in half lengthwise, then cut each half crosswise into eight wide strips. Twist each dough strip into a pretzel knot, then transfer the knots to the prepared trays and spread out in a single layer. Cover with dish towels and rest for 40 minutes at room temperature, or until doubled in size.

COMBINE the sugar and cinnamon, for coating the donuts, in a deep, heatproof bowl.

HEAT the oil in a deep, heavy-based saucepan over medium–high heat until it reaches 350°F. Deep-fry the donuts in batches, turning occasionally, for 2–3 minutes each, or until puffed, golden, and cooked through. Transfer to paper towels to drain briefly and, while still hot, gently roll in the cinnamon sugar to coat on all sides. Serve hot, warm, or at room temperature.

Donut and fruit kebabs

Donut shakers for boys and girls

Marshmallow chocolate donut whoopies

Cookies and cream donuts

Iced honey-cream donuts

Lamington donuts

Banana split donuts

Jelly star donuts

CHAPTER 3

FOR LITTLE KIDS
{AND BIG KIDS TOO}

DONUT AND FRUIT KEBABS

A great healthy twist on a treat that the kids will have lots of fun eating.

CAKE DONUTS

5 tablespoons + 2 teaspoons unsalted butter, at room temperature
½ cup superfine sugar
1 egg, at room temperature
1 egg yolk, at room temperature
1 teaspoon vanilla extract
¾ cup milk
4 cups self-rising flour, plus extra for dusting
A good pinch of fine sea salt
Vegetable, canola, or rice bran oil, for deep-frying

TO COAT

7 oz powdered orange candy, such as Pixy Stix or Fun Dip

TO SERVE

15 strawberries
4 kiwifruit, peeled, thickly sliced into rounds

CREAM the butter and sugar together in the bowl of a stand mixer for 3 minutes, or until pale and fluffy. Add the egg, egg yolk, vanilla extract, and milk, and mix until just combined.

SIFT the flour and salt over the mixture in the bowl. Mix until just combined, but do not overmix or the dough will become tough.

LIGHTLY flour a clean surface, turn the dough out onto it and, using lightly floured hands, gently bring together. Knead gently for a few seconds until the dough becomes smooth. Using a floured rolling pin, gently roll the dough out to a ⅓ inch thickness. Using a floured 1¾ inch round cookie cutter, cut out rounds from the dough, making sure you cut them as close together as possible. Re-roll any scraps and cut out more rounds until you have 30 in total.

HEAT the oil in a deep, heavy-based saucepan over medium–high heat until it reaches 350°F. Deep-fry the donuts in batches, turning occasionally, for 2–3 minutes each, or until puffed, golden, and cooked through. Transfer to paper towels to drain briefly, then allow to cool.

PUT the sherbet into a deep, heatproof bowl and gently toss and roll the donuts in the sherbet until coated on all sides. Using 15 wooden skewers, alternately thread two donuts, one strawberry, and one slice of kiwifruit onto each skewer, then serve.

DONUT SHAKERS FOR BOYS AND GIRLS

These donuts add a little fun to the kitchen — great for parties and keeping little hands busy.

CAKE DONUTS
5 tablespoons + 2 teaspoons
   unsalted butter, at room
   temperature
½ cup superfine sugar
1 egg, at room temperature
1 egg yolk, at room temperature
1 teaspoon vanilla extract
¾ cup milk
4 cups self-rising flour,
   plus extra for dusting
A good pinch of fine sea salt

TO COAT
3½ tablespoons unsalted butter
¾ cup honey

FAIRY DUST
5 oz edible sprinkles
1 tablespoon small silver dragees

OTHER DECORATIONS
⅓ cup small chocolate balls
⅓ cup chocolate sprinkles

CREAM the butter and sugar together in the bowl of a stand mixer for 3 minutes, or until pale and fluffy. Add the egg, egg yolk, vanilla extract, and milk and mix until just combined.

SIFT the flour and salt over the mixture in the bowl. Mix until just combined, but do not overmix or the dough will become tough.

LIGHTLY flour a clean surface, turn the dough out onto it and, using lightly floured hands, gently bring together. Knead gently for a few seconds until the dough becomes smooth. Using a floured rolling pin, gently roll the dough out to a ⅓ inch thickness. Using a floured 1⅛ inch round cookie cutter, cut out rounds from the dough, making sure you cut them as close together as possible. Re-roll any scraps and cut out more rounds until you have 80 in total.

PREHEAT the oven to 350°F. Line two large baking trays with parchment paper. Place the donuts about 1⅛ inches apart on the prepared trays.

BAKE each tray of donuts for 12–15 minutes, or until puffed, light golden, and cooked through (the donuts will sound hollow when the bases are tapped). Allow to cool on the trays for 3 minutes.

MEANWHILE, place the butter and honey together in a small saucepan over low heat, stir until the butter melts and the mixture is warm. Remove from the heat, transfer to a heatproof bowl, and cover to keep warm.

COMBINE the ingredients for the fairy dust and other decorations separately in different bowls. Divide the fairy dust between five paper bags and the other decorations between another five paper bags.

WORKING in batches, quickly toss the warm donuts in the warm melted butter mixture to coat on all sides. Using tongs, divide the donuts evenly between the shaker bags. Hand to children and allow them to shake vigorously to coat on all sides. Serve warm.

MARSHMALLOW CHOCOLATE DONUT WHOOPIES

A seriously decadent treat. The homemade marshmallow adds a gooey yum factor.

CAKE DONUT WHOOPIES

5 tablespoons + 2 teaspoons unsalted butter, at room temperature
½ cup superfine sugar
1 egg, at room temperature
1 egg yolk, at room temperature
1 teaspoon vanilla extract
¾ cup milk
4 cups self-rising flour, plus extra for dusting
A good pinch of fine sea salt
⅔ cup cocoa powder

MARSHMALLOW

¾ cup sugar
½ cup light corn syrup
2 egg whites, at room temperature
¼ teaspoon cream of tartar
2 teaspoons vanilla extract
12 drops red food coloring

TO SERVE

Confectioners' sugar, for dusting

CREAM the butter and sugar together in the bowl of a stand mixer for 3 minutes, or until pale and fluffy. Add the egg, egg yolk, vanilla extract, and milk and mix until just combined.

SIFT the flour, salt, and cocoa powder over the mixture in the bowl. Mix until just combined, but do not overmix or the dough will become tough.

LIGHTLY flour a clean surface, turn the dough out onto it and, using lightly floured hands, gently bring together. Knead gently for a few seconds until the dough becomes smooth. Using a floured rolling pin, gently roll the dough out to a ⅓ inch thickness. Using a floured 3½ inch round cookie cutter, cut out rounds from the dough, making sure you cut them as close together as possible. Re-roll any scraps and cut out more rounds until you have 12 in total.

PREHEAT the oven to 350°F. Line two large baking trays with parchment paper. Place the donuts about 1⅛ inches apart on the prepared trays.

BAKE each tray of donuts for 12–15 minutes, or until puffed, light golden, and cooked through (the donuts will sound hollow when the bases are tapped). Allow to cool completely on the trays. Halve the donuts by cutting horizontally through the center.

STIR the sugar, light corn syrup, and ¼ cup water for the marshmallow in a medium saucepan over high heat until the sugar has dissolved. Bring to a boil, and boil for 8–10 minutes, or until the mixture reaches 250°F on a sugar thermometer.

BEAT the egg whites and cream of tartar in the bowl of a stand mixer until soft peaks form, then with the motor running on medium speed, slowly add the hot sugar mixture in a thin steady stream. Once added, increase the speed to medium–high and beat for 8 minutes, or until the mixture is stiff and glossy. Beat in the vanilla extract and red food coloring.

USING two tablespoons, spoon the marshmallow mixture over the donut bases. Gently replace the donut tops, pushing down lightly (but do not allow the marshmallow to reach the edges because as it sets it will spread further). Leave the marshmallow to firm up, then lightly dust the tops with confectioners' sugar and serve.

COOKIES AND CREAM DONUTS

These addictive donuts will have the adults coming back for more, too.

YEAST DONUTS

1 cup lukewarm milk
3½ teaspoons dried yeast
3⅔ cups all-purpose flour,
    plus extra for dusting
¼ cup superfine sugar
A good pinch of fine sea salt
1 egg, at room temperature,
    lightly whisked
2 tablespoons unsalted butter,
    melted, at room temperature
Vegetable, canola, or rice bran
    oil, for deep-frying

TO SERVE

1 cup mini cream-filled chocolate
    cookies, such as mini Oreos,
    roughly crushed

CHOCOLATE CREAM ICING

1 cup confectioners' sugar
⅓ cup cocoa powder
⅓ cup whipping cream

COOKIE CREAM

2⅛ cups whipping cream
1½ cups mini cream-filled
    chocolate cookies, such as
    mini Oreos, finely crushed

WHISK the milk and yeast together in a small bowl. Add 1 teaspoon of the flour and 1 teaspoon of the sugar and whisk until well combined. Leave to stand at room temperature in a warm spot for 10–15 minutes, or until frothy.

PLACE the remaining flour, remaining sugar, and the salt in the bowl of a stand mixer. Attach the dough hook and mix together on medium speed until well combined.

WITH the motor running, slowly add the egg, melted butter, and the yeast mixture. Mix for 8 minutes, or until the dough is smooth and elastic (the dough should feel slightly sticky).

USING very lightly floured hands, scrape the dough into a lightly oiled bowl. Cover with a piece of parchment paper then a dish towel. Set aside to rest at room temperature in a warm, draft-free spot for 1–1½ hours, or until the dough has doubled in size.

LINE two large baking trays with parchment paper. Generously flour a work surface and gently tip the dough out onto it. Using a floured rolling pin, gently roll out to a ⅓ inch thickness. Using a floured 3½ inch round cookie cutter, cut out 10 rounds from the dough, making sure you cut them as close together as possible. Use a floured 1⅛ inch round cookie cutter to cut out holes from the center of each larger circle. Transfer the donuts to the prepared trays in a single layer. Cover with dish towels. Rest for 40 minutes at room temperature or until doubled in size.

HEAT the oil in a deep, heavy-based saucepan over medium–high heat until it reaches 350°F. Deep-fry the donuts in batches, turning occasionally, for 2–3 minutes each, or until puffed, golden, and cooked through. Transfer to paper towels to drain briefly, then allow to cool.

WHISK all the ingredients for the chocolate cream icing together until well combined and smooth. Spread the icing over the tops of the donuts, then transfer them to a wire rack set over a baking tray. Sprinkle with the roughly crushed cookies and leave to set.

FOR the cookie cream, beat the cream until soft peaks form, then fold through the crushed cookies. Spoon into a piping bag fitted with a ⅓ inch star tip. Pipe the cookie cream into the donut centers, then serve.

ICED HONEY-CREAM DONUTS

Little boys and girls alike will love these cute, honey-flavored treats.

YEAST DONUTS
1 cup lukewarm milk
3½ teaspoons dried yeast
3⅔ cups all-purpose flour,
    plus extra for dusting
¼ cup superfine sugar
A good pinch of fine sea salt
1 egg, at room temperature,
    lightly whisked
2 tablespoons unsalted butter,
    melted, at room temperature
Vegetable, canola, or rice bran
    oil, for deep-frying

HONEY CREAM
1¼ cups whipping cream
2 tablespoons honey

ICING
1 cup confectioners' sugar
3 teaspoons milk
6 drops pink food coloring
4 drops blue food coloring

TO DECORATE
White buttons
Twine

WHISK the milk and yeast together in a small bowl. Add 1 teaspoon of the flour and 1 teaspoon of the sugar and whisk until well combined. Allow to stand at room temperature in a warm spot for 10–15 minutes, or until frothy.

PLACE the remaining flour, remaining sugar, and the salt in the bowl of a stand mixer. Attach the dough hook and mix together on medium speed until well combined.

WITH the motor running, slowly add the egg, melted butter, and the yeast mixture. Mix for 8 minutes, or until the dough is smooth and elastic (the dough should feel slightly sticky).

USING very lightly floured hands, scrape the dough into a lightly oiled bowl. Cover with a piece of parchment paper, then a dish towel. Set aside to rest at room temperature in a warm, draft-free spot for 1–1½ hours or until the dough has doubled in size.

LINE two large baking trays with parchment paper. Generously flour a work surface, then tip the dough out onto it. Using a floured rolling pin, gently roll the dough out to a ⅓ inch thickness. Using a floured 2⅓ inch round cookie cutter, cut out 18 rounds, cutting them as close together as possible. Carefully transfer the donuts to the prepared trays, spreading them out in single layers and cover with dish towels. Rest for 40 minutes at room temperature, or until doubled in size.

HEAT the oil in a deep, heavy-based saucepan over medium–high heat until it reaches 350°F. Deep-fry the donuts in batches, turning occasionally, for 2–3 minutes each, or until puffed, golden, and cooked through. Transfer to paper towels to drain, then allow to cool.

BEAT the honey cream ingredients together in the bowl of a stand mixer until soft peaks form. Spoon into a piping bag fitted with a ¼ inch round tip.

WHISK the icing ingredients together in a bowl until well combined and smooth. Halve the mixture and stir pink food coloring through one half and blue food coloring through the remaining half.

PIPE the honey cream into the centers of the donuts. Transfer to a wire rack set over a baking tray. Spoon either pink or blue icing over the donuts and allow to set. Thread the buttons onto lengths of twine and use these to tie stacks of the donuts together before serving.

LAMINGTON DONUTS

A modern twist on an Australian classic, these are the perfect size for popping into your mouth.

YEAST DONUTS
1 cup lukewarm milk
3½ teaspoons dried yeast
3⅔ cups all-purpose flour, plus extra for dusting
¼ cup superfine sugar
A good pinch of fine sea salt
1 egg, at room temperature, lightly whisked
2 tablespoons unsalted butter, melted, at room temperature
Vegetable, canola, or rice bran oil, for deep-frying

LAMINGTON ICING
½ cup boiling water
4 tablespoons unsalted butter
2 cups confectioners' sugar
⅔ cup cocoa powder
3 cups desiccated coconut

WHISK the milk and yeast together in a small bowl. Add 1 teaspoon of the flour and 1 teaspoon of the sugar and whisk until well combined. Allow to stand at room temperature in a warm spot for 10–15 minutes, or until frothy.

PLACE the remaining flour, remaining sugar, and the salt in the bowl of a stand mixer. Attach the dough hook and mix together on medium speed until well combined.

WITH the motor running, slowly add the egg, melted butter, and the yeast mixture. Mix for 8 minutes, or until the dough is smooth and elastic (the dough should feel slightly sticky).

USING very lightly floured hands, scrape the dough into a lightly oiled bowl. Cover with a piece of parchment paper, then a dish towel. Set aside to rest at room temperature in a warm, draft-free spot for 1–1½ hours, or until the dough has doubled in size.

LINE two large baking trays with parchment paper. Generously flour a work surface and gently tip the dough out onto it. Using a floured rolling pin, gently roll the dough out to a ⅓ inch thickness. Using a floured 1¾ inch round cookie cutter, cut out 28 rounds from the dough, making sure you cut them as close together as possible. Carefully transfer the donuts to the prepared trays, spreading them out in a single layer. Cover with dish towels and rest for 40 minutes at room temperature, or until doubled in size.

HEAT the oil in a deep, heavy-based saucepan over medium–high heat until it reaches 350°F. Deep-fry the donuts in batches, turning occasionally, for 2–3 minutes each, or until puffed, golden, and cooked through. Transfer to paper towels to drain briefly, then allow to cool.

WHISK the water, butter, sugar, and cocoa for the Lamington icing together until well combined and smooth. Place the coconut in a bowl.

USING two forks, dip the donuts, one at a time, into the Lamington icing to coat on all sides. Allow the excess to drip off, then gently roll in the coconut to coat. Transfer to a wire rack set over a baking tray and allow to set before serving.

BANANA SPLIT DONUTS

A great weekend sweet treat that the whole family will love.

YEAST DONUTS

1 cup lukewarm milk
3½ teaspoons dried yeast
3⅔ cups all-purpose flour,
    plus extra for dusting
¼ cup superfine sugar
A good pinch of fine sea salt
1 egg, at room temperature,
    lightly whisked
2 tablespoons unsalted butter,
    melted, at room temperature
Vegetable, canola, or rice bran
    oil, for deep-frying

TO COAT

1 cup sugar
2 teaspoons ground cinnamon

TO SERVE

2 bananas, peeled, thinly sliced
⅓ cup finely chopped unsalted
    roasted peanuts
10 candied cherries

STRAWBERRY CREAM

1¼ cups whipping cream
½ cup strawberry jam

WHISK the milk and yeast together in a small bowl. Add 1 teaspoon of the flour and 1 teaspoon of the sugar and whisk until well combined. Allow to stand at room temperature in a warm spot for 10–15 minutes, or until frothy.

PLACE the remaining flour, remaining sugar, and the salt in the bowl of a stand mixer. Attach the dough hook and mix together on medium speed until well combined.

WITH the motor running, slowly add the egg, melted butter, and the yeast mixture. Mix for 8 minutes, or until the dough is smooth and elastic (the dough should feel slightly sticky).

USING very lightly floured hands, scrape the dough into a lightly oiled bowl. Cover with a piece of parchment paper then a dish towel. Set aside to rest at room temperature in a warm, draft-free spot for 1–1½ hours, or until the dough has doubled in size.

LINE two large baking trays with parchment paper. Generously flour a work surface then gently tip the dough out onto it. Using a floured rolling pin, gently roll the dough out to a ⅓ inch thick rectangle about 10 x 6 inches. Using a large floured knife, cut this rectangle in half lengthwise, then cut each piece into five wide strips crosswise to produce 10 smaller rectangles in total.

CAREFULLY transfer the donuts to the prepared trays, placing them about 2 inches apart in a single layer. Cover with dish towels and rest for 40 minutes at room temperature, or until doubled in size.

COMBINE the sugar and cinnamon in a deep, heatproof bowl.

HEAT the oil in a deep, heavy-based saucepan over medium–high heat until it reaches 350°F. Deep-fry the donuts in batches, turning occasionally, for 2–3 minutes each, or until puffed, golden, and cooked through. Transfer to paper towels to drain briefly. While hot, roll in the cinnamon sugar to coat on all sides, then allow to cool.

FOR the strawberry cream, beat the cream until firm peaks form, then stir through the jam until well combined. Slice the cooled donuts through the top lengthwise, creating a pocket for the cream, being careful not to cut all the way through. Spoon the strawberry cream down the length of each donut, then top with banana, nuts, and a candied cherry before serving.

JELLY STAR DONUTS

The jelly crystals add a sparkly touch to these donuts. You can use any flavor you like.

CAKE DONUT STARS

5 tablespoons + 2 teaspoons
    unsalted butter, at room
    temperature
½ cup superfine sugar
1 egg, at room temperature
1 egg yolk, at room temperature
1 teaspoon vanilla extract
¾ cup milk
4 cups self-rising flour,
    plus extra for dusting
A good pinch of fine sea salt
Vegetable, canola, or rice bran
    oil, for deep-frying

TO COAT

3 oz package strawberry-flavored
    gelatin "jello" crystals

CREAM the butter and sugar together in the bowl of a stand mixer for 3 minutes, or until pale and fluffy. Add the egg, egg yolk, vanilla extract, and milk and mix until just combined.

SIFT the flour and salt over the mixture in the bowl. Mix until just combined, but do not overmix or the dough will become tough.

LIGHTLY flour a clean surface, turn the dough out onto it and, using lightly floured hands, gently bring together. Knead gently for a few seconds until the dough becomes smooth. Using a floured rolling pin, gently roll the dough out to a ⅓ inch thickness. Using a floured 2⅓ inch star-shaped cookie cutter, cut out stars from the dough, making sure you cut them as close together as possible. Re-roll any scraps and cut out more stars until you have 28 in total.

PLACE the jelly crystals in a deep, heatproof bowl.

HEAT the oil in a deep, heavy-based saucepan over medium–high heat until it reaches 350°F. Deep-fry the donuts in batches, turning occasionally, for 2–3 minutes each, or until puffed, golden, and cooked through. Transfer to paper towels to drain briefly. While hot, toss the donuts in the jelly crystals to coat on all sides. Serve hot, warm, or at room temperature.

Cosmopolitan-cocktail donuts

Lime cheesecake donuts

Apple crumble donuts

Éclair croissant-donuts

Strawberry brûlée croissant-donuts

Croissant-donut bites with
dulce de leche

Lemon meringue donuts

After-dinner chocolate-mint donuts

CHAPTER 4

DONUTS FOR GROWN-UPS

COSMOPOLITAN-COCKTAIL DONUTS

This adults-only donut has a boozy icing that's fit for any cocktail party.

CAKE DONUTS

5 tablespoons + 2 teaspoons unsalted butter, at room temperature
½ cup superfine sugar
1 egg, at room temperature
1 egg yolk, at room temperature
1 teaspoon vanilla extract
¾ cup milk
4 cups self-rising flour, plus extra for dusting
A good pinch of fine sea salt
Vegetable, canola, or rice bran oil, for deep-frying

COSMOPOLITAN ICING

1 cup confectioners' sugar
2 teaspoons citron vodka
½ teaspoon Cointreau
1½ tablespoons cranberry cordial

TO SERVE

Orange zest
Pink dragees

CREAM the butter and sugar together in the bowl of a stand mixer for 3 minutes, or until pale and fluffy. Add the egg, egg yolk, vanilla extract, and milk and mix until just combined.

SIFT the flour and salt over the mixture in the bowl. Mix until just combined, but do not overmix or the dough will become tough.

LIGHTLY flour a clean surface, turn the dough out onto it and, using lightly floured hands, gently bring together. Knead gently for a few seconds until the dough becomes smooth. Using a floured rolling pin, gently roll the dough out to a ⅓ inch thickness. Using a floured 3½ inch round cookie cutter, cut out rounds from the dough, making sure you cut them as close together as possible. Re-roll any scraps and cut out more rounds until you have 12 in total. Use a floured 1⅛ inch round cookie cutter to cut out holes from the center of each larger circle.

HEAT the oil in a deep, heavy-based saucepan over medium–high heat until it reaches 350°F. Deep-fry the donuts in batches, turning occasionally, for 2–3 minutes each, or until puffed, golden, and cooked through. Transfer to paper towels to drain, then leave to cool.

MAKE the Cosmopolitan icing by whisking all of the ingredients together in a bowl until well combined and smooth.

SPREAD the icing over each donut, then transfer to a wire rack set over a baking tray. Decorate the tops with the orange zest and dragees. Allow to set and then serve.

LIME CHEESECAKE DONUTS

There is a wonderfully zingy taste of lime in this donut's cheesecake filling that makes for a great afternoon treat.

YEAST DONUTS
1 cup lukewarm milk
3½ teaspoons dried yeast
3⅔ cups all-purpose flour,
    plus extra for dusting
¼ cup superfine sugar
A good pinch of fine sea salt
1 egg, at room temperature,
    lightly whisked
2 tablespoons unsalted butter,
    melted, at room temperature
Vegetable, canola, or rice bran
    oil, for deep-frying

TO COAT
1 cup sugar
1 tablespoon finely grated
    lime zest

LIME CHEESECAKE FILLING
½ cup cream cheese
1 cup mascarpone cheese
2 tablespoons superfine sugar
2 teaspoons finely grated
    lime zest
⅓ cup freshly squeezed lime juice

WHISK the milk and yeast together in a small bowl. Add 1 teaspoon of the flour and 1 teaspoon of the sugar, then whisk until well combined. Allow to stand at room temperature in a warm spot for 10–15 minutes, or until frothy.

PLACE the remaining flour, remaining sugar, and the salt in the bowl of a stand mixer. Attach the dough hook and mix together on medium speed until well combined.

WITH the motor running, slowly add the egg, melted butter, and the yeast mixture. Mix for 8 minutes, or until the dough is smooth and elastic (the dough should feel slightly sticky).

USING very lightly floured hands, scrape the dough into a lightly oiled bowl. Cover with a piece of parchment paper, then a dish towel. Set aside to rest at room temperature in a warm, draft-free spot for 1–1½ hours, or until the dough has doubled in size.

LINE two large baking trays with parchment paper. Generously flour a work surface and gently tip the dough out onto it. Using a floured rolling pin, gently roll the dough out to a ⅓ inch thickness. Using a floured 2⅓ inch round cookie cutter, cut out 18 rounds from the dough, making sure you cut them as close together as possible. Carefully transfer the donuts to the prepared trays, spreading them out in a single layer. Cover with clean dish towels and leave to rest for 40 minutes at room temperature, or until they have doubled in size.

COMBINE the sugar and lime zest, for coating the donuts, in a deep, heatproof bowl.

HEAT the oil in a deep, heavy-based saucepan over medium–high heat, or until it reaches 350°F. Deep-fry the donuts in batches, turning occasionally, for 2–3 minutes each, or until they are puffed, golden, and cooked through. Transfer to paper towels to drain briefly then, while still hot, toss in the lime and sugar mixture to coat. Reserve any leftover lime sugar and leave the donuts to cool.

MAKE the lime cheesecake filling by beating the ingredients together in a bowl until well combined and smooth.

HALVE each donut horizontally through the center then spoon the filling into the middle of each donut base. Replace the tops and push down firmly. Sprinkle with some of the leftover lime sugar before serving.

APPLE CRUMBLE DONUTS

Reminiscent of a classic winter dessert, these donuts have all the charm of tradition, but with a modern twist.

CRUMBLE TOPPING

3½ tablespoons unsalted chilled butter, chopped
⅔ cup all-purpose flour
¼ cup firmly packed brown sugar
⅛ cup rolled oats
½ teaspoon pumpkin pie spice

CAKE DONUTS

5 tablespoons + 2 teaspoons unsalted butter, at room temperature
¼ cup superfine sugar
¼ cup applesauce
1 egg yolk, at room temperature
1 teaspoon vanilla extract
¾ cup milk
4 cups self-rising flour, plus extra for dusting
A good pinch of fine sea salt
Vegetable, canola, or rice bran oil, for deep-frying

APPLE GLAZE

1 cup confectioners' sugar
2–3 tablespoons apple juice

TO SERVE

2 large green apples
1 tablespoon lemon juice

PREHEAT the oven to 400°F. Line a baking tray with parchment paper. Pulse the butter and flour for the crumble together in a food processor until coarse crumbs form. Transfer to a bowl, then stir through the remaining crumble ingredients. Spread out evenly on a baking tray lined with parchment paper and bake for 10–12 minutes, or until crisp and golden. Allow to cool on the tray, then break into pieces.

CREAM the butter and sugar for the donuts together in the bowl of a stand mixer for 3 minutes, or until pale and fluffy. Add the applesauce, egg yolk, vanilla extract, and milk and mix until just combined.

SIFT the flour and salt over the mixture in the bowl. Mix until just combined, but do not overmix or the dough will become tough.

LIGHTLY flour a clean surface, turn the dough out onto it and, using lightly floured hands, gently bring together. Knead gently for a few seconds until the dough becomes smooth. Using a floured rolling pin, gently roll the dough out to a ⅓ inch thickness. Using a floured 3½ inch round cookie cutter, cut out rounds from the dough, making sure you cut them as close together as possible. Re-roll any scraps and cut out more rounds until you have 12 in total. Use a floured 1⅛ inch round cookie cutter to cut out holes from the center of each larger circle.

HEAT the oil in a deep, heavy-based saucepan over medium–high heat until it reaches 350°F. Deep-fry the donuts in batches for 2–3 minutes each, turning occasionally, or until cooked through, puffed, and golden. Transfer to paper towels to drain then allow to cool.

WHISK the ingredients for the apple glaze together in a bowl until well combined and smooth.

DIP the donuts, one at a time, into the glaze. Transfer to a wire rack set over a baking tray and allow to set.

THINLY slice the apples and seed them, then quickly toss them in lemon juice to keep them from browning. Use them to top the donuts, then sprinkle with the crumble topping and serve.

ÉCLAIR CROISSANT-DONUTS

A lovely twist on a French pastry — yet even more delightful for their perfect little size.

CROISSANT-DONUTS

¾ cup lukewarm milk
3 teaspoons dried yeast
¼ cup superfine sugar
2 eggs, at room temperature, lightly whisked
1 teaspoon vanilla extract
3⅔ cups all-purpose flour, plus extra for dusting
A good pinch of fine sea salt
Vegetable, canola, or rice bran oil, for deep-frying

BUTTER MIXTURE

¼ cup all-purpose flour
14 tablespoons unsalted butter, at room temperature

CHANTILLY CREAM

1¼ cups whipping cream
⅓ cup confectioners' sugar
2 teaspoons vanilla bean paste

TO SERVE

¾ cup milk chocolate chips, melted
⅓ cup raspberries, torn in half
Confectioners' sugar, for dusting

COMBINE the milk, yeast, sugar, eggs, vanilla extract, flour, and salt in the bowl of a stand mixer. Attach the dough hook and mix on low speed until the ingredients are well combined. Increase the speed to medium–low and mix for 4 minutes, or until the dough is smooth and elastic (the dough will be sticky). Line a baking tray with parchment paper and lightly flour it before transferring the dough onto the tray. Flatten to a rough 8 x 6 inches rectangle with lightly floured fingertips. Cover with another piece of parchment paper and refrigerate for 30 minutes.

BEAT the flour and butter for the butter mixture in the bowl of a stand mixer until smooth. Transfer the chilled dough and paper to a work surface and roll out to a ¼ inch thick rectangle roughly 12 x 8 inches. Spread the butter mixture evenly all over the dough, right to the edges. Fold the dough into thirds from the shorter sides, like a letter, then transfer back to the tray on the paper. Cover with parchment paper and refrigerate for 30 minutes.

REMOVE the dough from the fridge, transfer to a clean piece of parchment paper lightly dusted with flour, turn 90 degrees and roll into the same-sized rectangle again, then fold both edges to the middle. Refrigerate for 30 minutes, then repeat this turning, rolling, folding, and chilling sequence twice more. Finally, turn, roll, and fold the dough, then chill it for 1 hour.

LINE a large baking tray with parchment paper. Lightly flour a work surface. Roll the chilled dough out to a ¼ inch thick rectangle roughly 12 x 8 inches. Using a floured 2⅓ inch round cookie cutter, cut out 15 rounds from the dough, making sure you cut them as close together as possible. Carefully transfer to the prepared tray in a single layer. Cover with a dish towel. Rest for 40 minutes at room temperature or until they have doubled in size.

HEAT the oil in a deep, heavy-based saucepan over medium–high heat until it reaches 350°F. Deep-fry the croissant-donuts in batches for 2–3 minutes each, turning occasionally, or until puffed, golden, and cooked through. Transfer to paper towels to drain and allow to cool.

MAKE the chantilly cream by beating all of the ingredients together until soft peaks form. Spoon the mixture into a piping bag fitted with a ¼ inch round tip, then pipe the cream into the center of each croissant-donut. Top with melted chocolate, then raspberries. Dust lightly with confectioners' sugar and serve.

STRAWBERRY BRÛLÉE CROISSANT-DONUTS

These are perfect for a ladies' high tea. Make them during strawberry season for the best berry flavor.

CROISSANT-DONUTS

¾ cup lukewarm milk
3 teaspoons dried yeast
¼ cup superfine sugar
2 eggs, at room temperature, lightly whisked
1 teaspoon vanilla extract
3⅔ cups all-purpose flour, plus extra for dusting
A good pinch of fine sea salt
Vegetable, canola, or rice bran oil, for deep-frying

BUTTER MIXTURE

¼ cup all-purpose flour
14 tablespoons unsalted butter, at room temperature

TO COAT

1 cup sugar
2 teaspoons ground cinnamon

TO SERVE

3¼ cups strawberries, halved
1 tablespoon superfine sugar

COMBINE the milk, yeast, sugar, eggs, vanilla, flour, and salt in the bowl of a stand mixer. Attach the dough hook and mix on low speed until well combined. Increase the speed to medium–low and mix for 4 minutes or until the dough is smooth and elastic (the dough will be sticky).

LINE a baking tray with parchment paper and lightly flour it before transferring the dough onto the tray. Flatten to a rough 8 x 6 inches rectangle with lightly floured fingertips. Cover with another piece of parchment paper and refrigerate for 30 minutes.

BEAT the flour and butter in the bowl of a stand mixer until smooth. Roll the chilled dough out to a ¼ inch thick rectangle roughly 12 x 8 inches. Spread the butter mixture evenly all over the dough, right to the edges. Fold the dough into thirds from the shorter sides, like a letter, then transfer back to the tray on the paper. Cover with parchment paper and refrigerate for 30 minutes.

REMOVE the dough from the fridge, transfer to a clean piece of parchment paper lightly dusted with flour, turn 90 degrees, and roll it into the same-sized rectangle again, then fold both edges to the middle. Refrigerate for 30 minutes, then repeat this turning, rolling, folding, and chilling sequence twice more. Finally, turn, roll, and fold the dough, then chill it for 1 hour.

LINE a large baking tray with parchment paper. Lightly flour a work surface. Roll the chilled dough out to a ¼ inch thick rectangle roughly 12 x 8 inches. Using a floured 3½ inch round cookie cutter, cut out eight rounds from the dough, making sure you cut them as close together as possible. Use a floured 1⅛ inch round cookie cutter to cut out holes from the center of each larger circle. Carefully transfer to the prepared tray in a single layer. Cover with a dish towel and rest for 40 minutes at room temperature or until doubled in size. Combine the sugar and cinnamon in a deep, heatproof bowl.

HEAT the oil in a deep, heavy-based saucepan over medium–high heat until it reaches 350°F. Deep-fry the donuts in batches, turning occasionally, for 2–3 minutes each, or until puffed, golden, and cooked through. Transfer to paper towels to drain then, while still hot, toss in the cinnamon sugar to coat.

PLACE the strawberries, cut-side up, on a foil-lined tray. Sprinkle with the sugar, then use a kitchen blowtorch to caramelize. Allow to cool, then serve with the croissant-donuts.

CROISSANT-DONUT BITES WITH DULCE DE LECHE

Decadence to the next level! A platter of these deliciously addictive, sweet-and-salty bites won't last long.

CROISSANT-DONUT BITES
¾ cup lukewarm milk
3 teaspoons dried yeast
¼ cup superfine sugar
2 eggs, at room temperature, lightly whisked
1 teaspoon vanilla extract
3⅔ cups) all-purpose flour, plus extra for dusting
A good pinch of fine sea salt
Vegetable, canola, or rice bran oil, for deep-frying

BUTTER MIXTURE
¼ cup all-purpose flour
14 tablespoons unsalted butter, at room temperature

TO SERVE
1 cup dulce de leche
Pink sea salt flakes

COMBINE the milk, yeast, sugar, eggs, vanilla, flour, and salt in the bowl of a stand mixer. Attach the dough hook and mix on low speed until well combined. Increase the speed to medium–low and mix for 4 minutes or until the dough is smooth and elastic (the dough will be sticky). Line a baking tray with parchment paper and lightly flour it before transferring the dough onto the tray. Flatten to a rough 8 x 6 inches rectangle with lightly floured fingertips. Cover with another piece of parchment paper and refrigerate for 30 minutes.

BEAT the flour and butter for the butter mixture in the bowl of a stand mixer until smooth. Transfer the chilled dough and paper to a work surface and roll out to a ¼ inch thick rectangle roughly 12 x 8 inches. Spread the butter mixture evenly over the dough, right to the edges. Fold the dough in thirds from the shorter sides, like a letter, then transfer back to the tray on the paper. Cover with parchment paper and refrigerate for 30 minutes.

REMOVE the dough from the fridge, transfer to a clean piece of parchment paper lightly dusted with flour, turn 90 degrees, and roll it into the same-sized rectangle again, then fold both edges to the middle. Refrigerate for 30 minutes, then repeat this turning, rolling, folding, and chilling sequence twice more. Finally, turn, roll, and fold the dough, then chill it for 1 hour.

LINE a large baking tray with parchment paper. Lightly flour a work surface. Roll the chilled dough out to a ¼ inch thick rectangle roughly 12 x 8 inches. Using a floured 1⅛ inch round cookie cutter, cut out 44 rounds from the dough, making sure you cut them as close together as possible. Carefully transfer these bites to the prepared tray in a single layer. Cover with a dish towel. Rest for 40 minutes at room temperature or until doubled in size.

HEAT the oil in a deep, heavy-based saucepan over medium–high heat until it reaches 350°F. Deep-fry the bites in batches for 2–3 minutes each, turning occasionally, or until puffed, golden, and cooked through. Transfer to paper towels to drain briefly.

PLACE the bites onto a serving platter and spoon the dulce de leche into a small serving bowl. Dip the bites into the dulce de leche to coat, sprinkle with pink sea salt and serve hot, warm, or at room temperature.

LEMON MERINGUE DONUTS

With a touch of decorative meringue piping, these super-simple donuts are transformed into stunning works of art.

YEAST DONUTS

1 cup lukewarm milk
3½ teaspoons dried yeast
3⅔ cups all-purpose flour,
    plus extra for dusting
¼ cup superfine sugar
A good pinch of fine sea salt
1 egg, at room temperature,
    lightly whisked
2 tablespoons unsalted butter,
    melted, at room temperature
Vegetable, canola, or rice bran
    oil, for deep-frying
1 cup lemon curd

MERINGUE

4 egg whites, at room temperature
¾ cup superfine sugar

TO SERVE

2 tablespoons finely grated
    lemon zest

WHISK the milk and yeast together in a small bowl. Add 1 teaspoon of the flour and 1 teaspoon of the sugar, then whisk until well combined. Allow to stand at room temperature in a warm spot for 10–15 minutes, or until frothy.

PLACE the remaining flour, the sugar, and the salt in the bowl of a stand mixer. Attach the dough hook and mix on medium speed until well combined.

WITH the motor running, slowly add the egg, melted butter, and the yeast mixture. Mix for 8 minutes, or until the dough is smooth and elastic (the dough should feel slightly sticky).

USING very lightly floured hands, scrape the dough into a lightly oiled bowl. Cover with a piece of parchment paper, then a dish towel. Set aside to rest at room temperature in a warm, draft-free spot for 1–1½ hours, or until the dough has doubled in size.

LINE two large baking trays with parchment paper. Generously flour a work surface, then gently tip the dough out onto it. Using a floured rolling pin, gently roll the dough out to a ⅓ inch thickness. Using a floured 3½ inch round cookie cutter, cut out 10 rounds from the dough, making sure you cut them as close together as possible. Use a floured 1⅛ inch round cookie cutter to cut out holes from the center of each larger circle. Carefully transfer the donuts to the prepared trays in a single layer, then cover with dish towels. Rest for 40 minutes at room temperature, or until doubled in size.

HEAT the oil in a deep, heavy-based saucepan over medium–high heat until it reaches 350°F. Deep-fry the donuts in batches, turning occasionally, for 2–3 minutes each, or until puffed, golden, and cooked through. Transfer to paper towels to drain. Allow to cool.

CUT the donuts in half horizontally and spread the bases with lemon curd. Replace the tops and transfer to the prepared trays.

MAKE the meringue by beating the egg whites in the bowl of a stand mixer until soft peaks form. Gradually beat in the sugar until firm peaks form and the sugar dissolves. Spoon the meringue into a piping bag fitted with a ⅓ inch star tip. Pipe the meringue over the tops of the donuts. Using a kitchen blowtorch, caramelize the meringue tops, then sprinkle with the lemon zest. Serve warm.

AFTER-DINNER CHOCOLATE-MINT DONUTS

Impress your dinner-party guests with these easy-to-prepare treats.

YEAST DONUTS

1 cup lukewarm milk
3½ teaspoons dried yeast
3⅔ cups all-purpose flour,
    plus extra for dusting
¼ cup superfine sugar
A good pinch of fine sea salt
1 egg, at room temperature,
    lightly whisked
2 tablespoons unsalted butter,
    melted, at room temperature
Vegetable, canola, or rice bran
    oil, for deep-frying

CHOCOLATE ICING

1 cup confectioners' sugar
¼ cup cocoa powder
1–2 tablespoons boiling water

MINT DRIZZLE

½ cup confectioners' sugar
1½ teaspoons peppermint extract
3 teaspoons boiling water

WHISK the milk and yeast together in a small bowl. Add 1 teaspoon of the flour and 1 teaspoon of the sugar, then whisk until well combined. Allow to stand at room temperature in a warm spot for 10–15 minutes, or until frothy.

PLACE the remaining flour, the sugar, and the salt in the bowl of a stand mixer. Attach the dough hook and mix together on medium speed until well combined.

WITH the motor running, slowly add the egg, melted butter, and the yeast mixture. Mix for 8 minutes, or until the dough is smooth and elastic (the dough should feel slightly sticky).

USING very lightly floured hands, scrape the dough into a lightly oiled bowl. Cover with a piece of parchment paper, then a dish towel. Set aside to rest at room temperature in a warm, draft-free spot for 1–1½ hours, or until the dough has doubled in size.

LINE two large baking trays with parchment paper. Generously flour a work surface then gently tip the dough out onto it. Using a floured rolling pin, gently roll the dough out to a ⅓ inch thickness. Using a floured 2⅓ inch round cookie cutter, cut out 18 rounds from the dough, making sure you cut them as close together as possible. Use the tip of a floured chopstick to push a hole through the center of each donut. Carefully transfer the donuts to the prepared trays, spreading them out in a single layer. Cover with dish towels. Rest for 40 minutes at room temperature, or until doubled in size. Re-open the center holes using a chopstick, if needed.

HEAT the oil in a deep, heavy-based saucepan over medium–high heat until it reaches 350°F. Deep-fry the donuts in batches, turning occasionally, for 2–3 minutes each, or until puffed, golden, and cooked through. Transfer to paper towels to drain, then allow to cool.

MAKE the icing by whisking all of the ingredients together in a bowl until well combined and smooth. Spread each donut with the chocolate icing, then transfer to a wire rack set over a baking tray. Allow to set.

WHISK all the ingredients for the mint drizzle together in a bowl until well combined and smooth. Spoon into a small re-sealable food storage bag. Snip one of the bottom corners off the bag and drizzle this mixture over the tops of the donuts. Allow to set, then serve.

Sugar-free orange donuts

Supergreens donuts

Salted caramel vegan donuts

Coconut and date paleo donuts

Raw superfood donuts

Gluten-free mocha donuts

CHAPTER 5

ALMOST GOOD FOR YOU

SUGAR-FREE ORANGE DONUTS

These donuts contain rice malt syrup, which is made from fermented cooked rice and is much better for you than sugar, as it is fructose-free and full of slow-releasing energy.

YEAST DONUTS
½ cup lukewarm water
3½ teaspoons dried yeast
3⅔ cups all-purpose flour,
    plus extra for dusting
A good pinch of fine sea salt
1 egg, at room temperature,
    lightly whisked
2 tablespoons unsalted butter,
    melted, at room temperature
½ cup freshly squeezed
    orange juice

ORANGE BUTTER
10½ tablespoons unsalted butter,
    at room temperature
¼ cup rice malt syrup
1 tablespoon finely grated
    orange zest

TO SERVE
1 orange, peeled and segmented
Rice malt syrup, to drizzle

WHISK the water and yeast together in a small bowl. Add 1 teaspoon of the flour and whisk until well combined. Allow to stand at room temperature in a warm spot for 10–15 minutes, or until frothy.

PLACE the remaining flour and the salt in the bowl of a stand mixer. Attach the dough hook and mix together on medium speed until well combined.

WITH the motor running, slowly add the egg, butter, orange juice, and then the yeast mixture. Mix for 8 minutes, or until the dough is smooth and elastic (the dough should feel slightly sticky).

USING very lightly floured hands, scrape the dough into a lightly oiled bowl. Cover with a piece of parchment paper then a dish towel. Set aside to rest at room temperature in a warm, draft-free spot for 1–1½ hours, or until the dough has doubled in size.

LINE two large baking trays with parchment paper. Generously flour a work surface and gently tip the dough out onto it. Using a floured rolling pin, gently roll the dough out to a ⅓ inch thickness. Using a floured 3½ inch round cookie cutter, cut out 10 rounds from the dough, making sure you cut them as close together as possible. Use a floured 1⅛ inch round cookie cutter to cut out holes from the center of each larger circle. Carefully transfer the donuts to the prepared trays, spreading them out in a single layer. Cover with dish towels, then leave to rest for 40 minutes at room temperature or until doubled in size.

PREHEAT the oven to 350°F. Line two large baking trays with parchment paper. Place the donuts about 1⅛ inches apart on the prepared trays.

BAKE each tray of donuts for 10–12 minutes, or until puffed, light golden, and cooked through (the donuts will sound hollow when the bases are tapped). Allow to cool completely on the trays.

BEAT the butter for the orange butter for 3 minutes or until very pale and fluffy, then add the remaining ingredients and beat until well combined.

SPREAD the orange butter over the donuts and transfer to a wire rack set over a baking tray. Top each donut with an orange segment. Drizzle with rice malt syrup before serving.

SUPERGREENS DONUTS

Topping these donuts with some deliciously sweet kale chips not only makes them look gorgeous, but they'll taste great, too.

HONEYED KALE CHIPS
2 large kale leaves, stems removed and discarded, leaves torn into 1⅛ inch pieces
2 tablespoons honey

CAKE DONUTS
5 tablespoons + 2 teaspoons unsalted butter, at room temperature
½ cup superfine sugar
1 egg, at room temperature
1 egg yolk, at room temperature
1 teaspoon vanilla extract
¾ cup milk
4 cups self-rising flour, plus extra for dusting
A good pinch of fine sea salt
2 teaspoons supergreens powder (see tip)

TO SERVE
Honey, to drizzle

PREHEAT the oven to 350°F. Line a large baking tray with parchment paper and arrange the torn kale leaves on the tray. Drizzle the honey all over the leaves and bake for 8–10 minutes, or until the leaves are crisp and golden around the edges. Allow to cool on the tray.

MEANWHILE, cream the butter and sugar together in a stand mixer for 3 minutes, or until pale and fluffy. Add the egg, egg yolk, vanilla extract, and milk and mix until just combined.

SIFT the flour and salt over the mixture in the bowl. Add the supergreens powder and mix until just combined, but do not overmix or the dough will become tough. The supergreens powder will give the dough a marbled effect.

LIGHTLY flour a clean surface, turn the dough out onto it and, using lightly floured hands, gently bring it together. Knead gently for a few seconds until the dough becomes smooth. Using a floured rolling pin, gently roll the dough out to a ⅓ inch thickness. Using a floured 3½ inch round cookie cutter, cut out rounds from the dough, making sure you cut them as close together as possible. Re-roll any scraps and cut out more rounds until you have 12 in total. Use a floured 1⅛ inch round cookie cutter to cut out holes from the center of each larger circle.

LINE two large baking trays with parchment paper. Place the donuts 1⅛ inches apart on the prepared trays.

BAKE each tray of donuts in the oven for 12–15 minutes, or until puffed, light golden, and cooked through (the donuts will sound hollow when the bases are tapped). Cool for 3 minutes on the tray.

DRIZZLE the donuts generously with honey, then top with the honeyed kale chips. Serve hot, warm, or at room temperature.

TIP SUPERGREENS POWDER IS AVAILABLE FROM HEALTH FOOD STORES AND SOME SUPERMARKETS.

SALTED CARAMEL VEGAN DONUTS

This salted caramel sugar topping gives these donuts a sweet–salty punch of flavor.

CAKE DONUTS

5 tablespoons + 2 teaspoons
   dairy-free margarine spread,
   at room temperature
½ cup superfine sugar
¼ cup applesauce
1 teaspoon vanilla extract
¾ cup almond milk
4 cups self-rising flour,
   plus extra for dusting
A good pinch of fine sea salt

SALTED CARAMEL SUGAR

½ cup superfine sugar
½ cup firmly packed dark brown
   sugar
2 teaspoons fine sea salt

CREAM the margarine spread and sugar together in the bowl of a stand mixer for 3 minutes, or until pale and fluffy. Add the applesauce, vanilla extract, and milk and mix until just combined.

SIFT the flour and salt over the mixture in the bowl. Mix until just combined, but do not overmix or the dough will become tough.

LIGHTLY flour a clean surface, turn the dough out onto it and, using lightly floured hands, gently bring it together. Knead gently for a few seconds until the dough becomes smooth. Using a floured rolling pin, gently roll the dough out to a ⅓ inch thickness. Using a floured 3½ inch round cookie cutter, cut out rounds from the dough, making sure you cut them as close together as possible. Re-roll any scraps and cut out more rounds until you have 12 in total. Use a floured 1⅛ inch round cookie cutter to cut out holes from the center of each larger circle.

WHISK the ingredients for the salted caramel sugar together until well combined.

HEAT the oil in a deep, heavy-based saucepan over medium–high heat until it reaches 350°F. Deep-fry the donuts in batches, turning occasionally, for 2–3 minutes each, or until puffed, golden, and cooked through. Transfer to paper towels to drain briefly. While still hot, roll in the salted caramel sugar to coat on all sides. Serve hot, warm, or at room temperature.

COCONUT AND DATE PALEO DONUTS

These delicate donuts are grain-free and best served on the day of baking.

PALEO DONUTS
about 14 fresh dates,
    such as deglet noor
Boiling water, for soaking
¼ cup coconut oil, softened
3 eggs, at room temperature
½ cup coconut flour
½ cup almond meal

TO SERVE
2 tablespoons maple syrup
¼ cup desiccated coconut

PREHEAT the oven to 350°F. Grease 10 holes of a 12-hole non-stick donut pan.

SOAK the dates in boiling water for 15 minutes then drain. Remove their pits and pulse the flesh in a food processor until almost smooth.

STIR the coconut oil, eggs, coconut flour, almond meal, date mixture, and ¼ cup water together in a bowl until well combined and smooth. Spoon this mixture evenly into the prepared pan. Using your fingertips, press the mixture down firmly so you have a level surface. Bake for 15 minutes, or until the donuts are golden and firm when lightly pressed. Cool in the pan for 3 minutes, then transfer to a wire rack set over a baking tray.

BRUSH the warm donuts generously with maple syrup and sprinkle with the desiccated coconut. Serve warm or at room temperature.

TIP PALEO REFERS TO FOODS THAT WERE AVAILABLE IN THE PALEOLITHIC (CAVEMAN) ERA: NOTHING PROCESSED, ONLY NATURAL INGREDIENTS.

RAW SUPERFOOD DONUTS

A super-rich chocolate treat — enjoy these straight from the fridge! Make a big batch, as they keep well.

SUPERFOOD DONUTS

½ cup coconut oil, melted
⅔ cup raw cacao powder
2 tablespoons maca powder
½ cup rice malt syrup
⅓ cup chia seeds
2 tablespoons LSA mix (linseed, sunflower, and almond meal), available at most health food stores and online
2 tablespoons whole psyllium husks
2 tablespoons pepitas (pumpkin seeds)
2 tablespoons dried goji berries

TO COAT

Cacao nibs

GREASE a 12-hole non-stick donut pan.

STIR all the ingredients for the donuts together in a bowl until well combined.

SPOON this mixture evenly into the prepared pan. Using only your fingertips, press the mixture down firmly so you have a level surface.

COVER the pan with a dish towel and refrigerate for 30 minutes, or until the donut mix has almost set firm. Using a small palette knife, carefully remove the donuts from the pan. Roll them in cacao nibs, pressing down on the donuts for the nibs to adhere, until coated on all sides. Transfer the donuts to a baking tray lined with parchment paper. Cover and chill for another hour, or until set firm. Serve chilled.

TIP THESE DONUTS WILL SOFTEN IF LEFT AT ROOM TEMPERATURE, SO SERVE THEM STRAIGHT FROM THE FRIDGE. THEY'LL KEEP IN AN AIRTIGHT CONTAINER IN THE FRIDGE FOR UP TO TWO WEEKS AND CAN ALSO BE KEPT IN THE FREEZER FOR UP TO ONE MONTH. SERVE AS A FROZEN TREAT ON HOT DAYS.

GLUTEN-FREE MOCHA DONUTS

These are perfect for a breakfast treat, or as a pick-me-up in the afternoon.

CAKE DONUTS

5 tablespoons + 2 teaspoons unsalted butter, at room temperature

½ cup superfine sugar

1 egg, at room temperature

1 egg yolk, at room temperature

1 teaspoon vanilla extract

¾ cup milk

4 cups gluten-free self-rising flour, plus extra for dusting

¼ cup cocoa powder

A good pinch of fine sea salt

1 tablespoon instant coffee granules

Vegetable, canola, or rice bran oil, for deep-frying

MOCHA SUGAR

1½ teaspoons instant coffee granules

1 cup sugar

3 teaspoons cocoa powder

CREAM the butter and sugar together in the bowl of a stand mixer for 3 minutes, or until pale and fluffy. Add the egg, egg yolk, vanilla extract, and milk and mix until just combined.

SIFT the flour, cocoa, and salt over the mixture in the bowl. Add the instant coffee granules and mix until just combined, but do not overmix or the dough will become tough.

LIGHTLY flour a clean surface, turn the dough out onto it and, using lightly floured hands, gently bring together. Knead gently for a few seconds until the dough becomes smooth. Using a floured rolling pin, gently roll the dough out to a ⅓ inch thickness. Using a floured 3½ inch round cookie cutter, cut out rounds from the dough, making sure you cut them as close together as possible. Re-roll any scraps and cut out more rounds until you have 12 in total. Use a floured 1⅛ inch round cookie cutter to cut out holes from the center of each larger circle.

USE a mortar and pestle to grind the instant coffee granules for the mocha sugar to a fine powder. Combine the ground instant coffee granules, sugar, and cocoa powder in a deep, heatproof bowl.

HEAT the oil in a deep, heavy-based saucepan over medium–high heat until it reaches 350°F. Deep-fry the donuts in batches, turning occasionally, for 2–3 minutes each, or until puffed, golden, and cooked through. Transfer to paper towels to drain briefly then, while still hot, toss in the mocha sugar to coat on all sides. Serve hot, warm, or at room temperature.

TIP AS ALL BRANDS OF GLUTEN-FREE SELF-RISING FLOUR DIFFER IN TEXTURE, YOU MAY FIND THAT YOU NEED TO ADD A LITTLE MORE FLOUR OR A LITTLE MORE MILK TO GET THE DOUGH JUST RIGHT (THE CONSISTENCY SHOULD BE SOFT AND PLIABLE, NOT STICKY).

Sufganiyot (Israeli jam donuts)

Zeppole (Italian donuts)

Jalebi (Indian spiced donuts)

Loukoumades (Greek honey donuts)

Churros with chocolate dipping sauce

Sfenj (Moroccan donuts)

Pets de nonne (nun's farts)

Oliebollen (Dutch fruit donuts)

Youtiao (Chinese donuts)

Persians (pink-iced Canadian donuts)

CHAPTER 6

AROUND THE WORLD

SUFGANIYOT ISRAELI JAM DONUTS

A delicious jam-filled donut eaten in Israel and enjoyed throughout the world during Chanukah celebrations.

SUFGANIYOT

½ cup lukewarm water
2 teaspoons dried yeast
3⅔ cups all-purpose flour,
    plus extra for dusting
¼ cup superfine sugar
A good pinch of fine sea salt
1 teaspoon finely grated
    orange zest
2 egg yolks, at room temperature
1 egg, at room temperature
½ teaspoon vanilla extract
6 tablespoons unsalted butter,
    chopped
Vegetable, canola, or rice bran
    oil, for deep-frying

TO SERVE

1 cup strawberry jam
Confectioners' sugar, for dusting

WHISK the water and yeast together in a small bowl. Add 1 teaspoon of the flour and 1 teaspoon of the sugar and whisk until well combined. Allow to stand at room temperature in a warm spot for 10–15 minutes, or until frothy.

PLACE the remaining flour, remaining sugar, and the salt in the bowl of a stand mixer. Attach the dough hook and mix together on medium speed until well combined.

WITH the motor running, slowly add the orange zest, egg yolks, egg, vanilla extract, and then the yeast mixture. Mix for 4 minutes, or until well combined. Add the butter, a piece at a time, mixing for 4 minutes until the dough is smooth and elastic (it should feel slightly sticky).

USING very lightly floured hands, scrape the dough into a lightly oiled bowl. Cover with a piece of parchment paper, then a dish towel. Set aside to rest at room temperature in a warm, draft-free spot for 1–1½ hours, or until the dough has doubled in size.

LINE two large baking trays with parchment paper. Generously flour a work surface and gently tip the dough out onto it. Using a floured rolling pin, gently roll the dough out to a ⅓ inch thickness. Using a floured 2⅓ inch round cookie cutter, cut out 18 rounds from the dough, making sure you cut them as close together as possible. Carefully transfer the sufganiyot to the prepared trays, spreading them out in a single layer. Cover with dish towels. Rest for 40 minutes at room temperature, or until doubled in size.

HEAT the oil in a deep, heavy-based saucepan over medium–high heat until it reaches 350°F. Deep-fry the sufganiyot in batches, turning occasionally, for 2–3 minutes each, or until puffed, golden, and cooked through. Transfer to paper towels to drain briefly, then allow to cool.

PULSE the jam in a food processor until smooth, then spoon it into a piping bag fitted with a ¼ inch round tip. Pipe the jam into the centers of the sufganiyot, then dust generously with confectioners' sugar and serve.

 ITALIAN DONUTS

The dough of this southern Italian donut is enriched with fresh ricotta, making it beautifully soft and delicate.

ZEPPOLE

1¼ cups self-rising flour
A good pinch of fine sea salt
1 tablespoon granulated sugar
1 cup ricotta cheese
2 eggs, at room temperature, lightly whisked
1 teaspoon vanilla extract
Vegetable, canola, or rice bran oil, for deep-frying

TO SERVE

Confectioners' sugar, for dusting

COMBINE the flour, salt, sugar, ricotta, eggs, and vanilla extract in a bowl. Stir until the mixture is well combined (it should create a sticky batter).

HEAT the oil in a deep, heavy-based saucepan over medium–high heat until it reaches 350°F. Using an oiled spoon, carefully drop tablespoons of the dough into the hot oil. Deep-fry the zeppole in batches, turning occasionally, for 2–3 minutes each, or until they are puffed, golden, and cooked through.

TRANSFER to paper towels to drain briefly. Dust generously with confectioners' sugar and serve warm.

JALEBI INDIAN SPICED DONUTS

These super-sweet Indian treats are submerged in saffron syrup, which gives them a beautifully pale orange color.

JALEBI
1¼ cups all-purpose flour
½ cup plain yogurt
A good pinch of baking soda
Ghee (clarified butter), vegetable, canola, or rice bran oil, for deep-frying

SAFFRON SYRUP
1 cup sugar
½ teaspoon saffron threads

WHISK the flour, yogurt, and ¾ cup water together in a bowl until well combined and smooth. Whisk in the baking soda until well combined.

SPOON the batter into a piping bag fitted with a ¼ inch round tip, then place in the refrigerator and chill until required.

PLACE the sugar and ½ cup water for the saffron syrup in a small saucepan over high heat. Stir gently until the sugar dissolves, then bring to a boil for 2 minutes, or until slightly reduced. Remove the pan from the heat, stir in the saffron threads, then cover to keep warm.

WHEN ready to cook, heat the ghee or oil in a deep, heavy-based saucepan over medium–high heat until it reaches 350°F. Carefully pipe the chilled batter into the hot ghee or oil, forming concentric circles so each jalebi is about 3½ inches wide. Deep-fry the jalebi in batches, turning occasionally, for 2–3 minutes each, or until lightly puffed, golden, and cooked through.

TRANSFER to paper towels to drain briefly, then submerge the hot jalebi in the warm saffron syrup. Using a slotted spoon, remove them from the syrup and allow any excess to drain away. Transfer to a serving platter and serve warm.

 GREEK HONEY DONUTS

These syrup-drenched Greek donuts are served warm, and lightly dusted with cinnamon.

LOUKOUMADES
¼ cup lukewarm water,
    plus ¾ cup extra
1 teaspoon dried yeast
2 teaspoons superfine sugar
2⅛ cups all-purpose flour
A good pinch of fine sea salt
½ teaspoon vanilla extract
Vegetable, canola, or rice bran
    oil, for deep-frying

HONEY SYRUP
⅓ cup honey

TO SERVE
Ground cinnamon, for dusting

WHISK the ¼ cup water and yeast together in a large bowl. Add the sugar and 1 teaspoon of the flour and whisk until well combined. Allow to stand at room temperature in a warm spot for 10–15 minutes, or until frothy.

ADD the remaining flour, the salt, vanilla extract, and the extra ¾ cup water to the yeast mixture. Stir until well combined and smooth. Cover the bowl with a piece of parchment paper, then a dish towel and set aside to rest in a warm, draft-free spot for 1–1½ hours, or until the dough has doubled in size.

PLACE the honey for the honey syrup in a small saucepan over high heat with ½ cup water. Bring to a boil, then remove the pan from the heat and allow the syrup to cool in the pan.

LINE two large baking trays with parchment paper.

HEAT the oil in a deep, heavy-based saucepan over medium–high heat until it reaches 350°F. Using an oiled tablespoon, carefully drop spoonfuls of the batter into the hot oil. Deep-fry in batches, turning occasionally, for 2–3 minutes each, or until the loukoumades are puffed, golden, and cooked through. Drain briefly on paper towels, then transfer to the prepared trays.

DRIZZLE with the honey syrup, dust with cinnamon, and serve warm.

CHURROS WITH CHOCOLATE DIPPING SAUCE

These Spanish donuts are irresistible when served warm with this decadent chocolate dipping sauce. Delicious in the morning with coffee, or in the evening as a luxurious dessert.

CHURROS
4½ tabelspoons unsalted
    butter, chopped
1¼ cups all-purpose flour
¼ teaspoon salt
2 eggs, at room temperature
Vegetable, canola, or rice bran
    oil, for deep-frying

TO COAT
1 cup sugar
2 teaspoons ground cinnamon

CHOCOLATE DIPPING SAUCE
7 oz (about 8 squares)
    good-quality dark chocolate,
    coarsely chopped
1¼ cups light cream

PLACE the butter and 1 cup water together in a medium saucepan over high heat. Bring to a boil, stirring until the butter melts. Add the flour and salt and stir vigorously for 1 minute, or until the mixture comes together in a ball. Remove from the heat.

TRANSFER the flour mixture to the bowl of a stand mixer. Allow to stand for 10 minutes to cool slightly, then attach the paddle and beat on medium speed for 3 minutes. Add the eggs, one at a time, beating well between each addition, until the mixture is combined and glossy.

SPOON the dough into a piping bag fitted with a ⅓ inch star tip.

COMBINE the sugar and cinnamon, for coating the churros, in a deep, heatproof bowl.

PLACE the chopped chocolate and cream for the chocolate sauce in a heatproof bowl set over a saucepan of simmering water. Make sure the base of the bowl is not touching the water in the pan. Stir gently until the mixture melts together and is smooth. Remove the pan from the heat and set aside (keep the bowl set over the pan so the sauce stays warm).

HEAT the oil in a deep, heavy-based saucepan over medium–high heat until it reaches 350°F. Carefully pipe 3½ inch lengths of dough into the hot oil. Deep-fry in batches, turning occasionally, for 2–3 minutes each, or until the churros are puffed, golden, and cooked through. Transfer to paper towels to drain briefly then, while still hot, toss the churros in the cinnamon sugar to coat on all sides. Serve warm with the warm chocolate dipping sauce.

SFENJ — MOROCCAN DONUTS

These donuts are made from unsweetened dough, and once cooked, can be rolled in sugar or confectioners' sugar.

SFENJ
1 cup lukewarm water
1 tablespoon dried yeast
2 tablespoons sugar
3⅔ cups all-purpose flour,
    plus extra for dusting
A good pinch of fine sea salt

TO COAT
1 cup sugar

WHISK the water and yeast together in the bowl of a stand mixer. Add the sugar and 1 teaspoon of the flour, then whisk until well combined. Allow to stand in a warm spot for 10–15 minutes, or until frothy.

ADD the remaining flour and the salt to the yeast mixture. Attach the dough hook and mix on medium speed until well combined, then mix for 8 minutes more, or until the dough is smooth and elastic (the dough will feel firm).

GENEROUSLY oil a large bowl. Add the dough and turn to coat (it needs to be coated on all sides as this will prevent a crust from forming on the dough). Cover with plastic wrap, then a dish towel and set aside to rest in a warm, draft-free spot for 1–1½ hours, or until the dough has doubled in size. Press the dough down with the palms of your hands to expel some of the air.

HEAT the oil in a deep, heavy-based saucepan over medium–high heat until it reaches 350°F.

LIGHTLY dust a clean surface with flour then divide the dough into 12 equal portions. Knead each portion until smooth, flatten into 2⅓ inch rounds in your palms, then push a finger through the center to create a hole. Twirl the dough on your finger to enlarge the hole to the size of a tennis ball.

PLACE the sugar for coating in a deep, heatproof bowl.

DEEP-FRY the sfenj in batches, turning occasionally, for 2–3 minutes each, or until they are puffed, golden, and cooked through. Transfer to paper towels to drain briefly then, while still hot, toss in sugar to coat on all sides. Serve warm.

PETS DE NONNE NUN'S FARTS

These little French donuts are surprisingly light and airy, which helps explain their irreverent but fun name.

PETS DE NONNE

4 tablespoons unsalted
    butter, chopped
A good pinch of fine sea salt
⅔ cup all-purpose flour
2 eggs, at room temperature
Vegetable, canola, or rice bran
    oil, for deep-frying

TO SERVE

Confectioners' sugar, for dusting

PLACE the butter and ½ cup water in a saucepan over high heat. Bring to a boil, stirring until the butter melts. Add the salt and flour and stir vigorously for 1 minute, or until the mixture comes together in a ball. Remove from the heat.

TRANSFER the flour mixture to the bowl of a stand mixer. Allow to stand for 10 minutes to cool slightly, then attach the paddle and beat on medium speed for 3 minutes. Add the eggs, one at a time, beating well between each addition, until the mixture is well combined and glossy (it should be soft and sticky).

HEAT the oil in a deep, heavy-based saucepan over medium–high heat until it reaches 350°F. Using an oiled teaspoon, carefully drop heaped teaspoons of the dough into the hot oil. Deep-fry the *pets de nonne* in batches, turning occasionally, for 2–3 minutes each, or until puffed, golden, and cooked through. Transfer to paper towels to drain, then allow to cool. Dust generously with confectioners' sugar before serving.

OLIEBOLLEN — DUTCH FRUIT DONUTS

Traditionally eaten by the Dutch on New Year's Eve (and enjoyed in Belgium, too), these fruit-filled delicacies are affectionately known as "dutchies" elsewhere in the world.

OLIEBOLLEN
¼ cup lukewarm water
2 teaspoons dried yeast
2 tablespoons sugar
1¾ cups all-purpose flour
A good pinch of fine sea salt
½ cup milk
1 egg, at room temperature, lightly whisked
¼ cup currants
⅓ cup raisins
1 small green apple, peeled, cored, finely chopped
Vegetable, canola, or rice bran oil, for deep-frying

TO SERVE
Confectioners' sugar, for dusting

WHISK the water and yeast together in a large bowl. Add the sugar and whisk until well combined. Allow to stand in a warm spot for 10–15 minutes, or until frothy.

ADD the flour, salt, milk, egg, currants, raisins, and apple to the yeast mixture. Stir until well combined, then cover with a piece of parchment paper and a dish towel. Set aside to rest in a warm, draft-free spot for 1–1½ hours, or until the dough has doubled in size (the mixture will be soft and sticky).

HEAT the oil in a deep, heavy-based saucepan over medium–high heat until it reaches 350°F. Using an oiled tablespoon, carefully drop spoonfuls of the dough into the hot oil. Deep-fry the oliebollen in batches, turning occasionally, for 2–3 minutes each, or until puffed, golden, and cooked through.

TRANSFER to paper towels to drain briefly. Dust generously with confectioners' sugar and serve warm.

YOUTIAO CHINESE DONUTS

Also known as Chinese oil sticks, these are eaten piping hot and crispy alongside savory rice dishes, or used for dipping into hot coffee or chocolate.

YOUTIAO

4 cups all-purpose flour, plus extra for dusting
1 teaspoon dried yeast
1 teaspoon baking powder
1 teaspoon fine sea salt
2 tablespoons sugar
1½ cups lukewarm water
Vegetable, canola, or rice bran oil, for deep-frying

PLACE all of the ingredients for the youtiao in the bowl of a stand mixer. Attach the dough hook and mix together on medium speed until well combined, then mix for 5 minutes more, or until the dough is smooth and elastic (the dough will feel slightly sticky).

TRANSFER the dough to a lightly oiled bowl, cover with a piece of parchment paper, then a dish towel. Set aside to rest in a warm, draft-free spot for 1–1½ hours, or until the dough has doubled in size.

LINE two large baking trays with parchment paper. Generously flour a work surface and gently tip the dough out onto it. Using a floured rolling pin, roll the dough out to a ¼ inch thick, 16 x 8 inches rectangle. Using a large floured knife, cut the dough into ¾ inch wide strips crosswise until you have 40 strips. Wet a finger in a bowl of water, then run it down the length of a strip and place another strip on top, pressing down lightly to seal them together. Transfer to a prepared tray, then repeat until you have used up the rest of the dough. Allow to rest for 15 minutes at room temperature, or until the sticks are slightly puffed up.

HEAT the oil in a deep, heavy-based frying pan over medium–high heat until it reaches 350°F. Deep-fry the youtiao in batches, turning occasionally, for 2–3 minutes each, or until puffed, golden, and cooked through.

TRANSFER to paper towels to drain briefly, then serve hot.

 PINK-ICED CANADIAN DONUTS

Originating in the city of Thunder Bay, Canada, these sweet cinnamon scroll donuts are topped with icing made from fresh raspberries and sometimes strawberries.

PERSIANS
2 tablespoons lukewarm water, plus ½ cup extra
2 teaspoons dried yeast
¼ cup superfine sugar
¼ teaspoon fine sea salt
1 teaspoon ground cinnamon
2 teaspoons vanilla extract
1 egg, at room temperature, lightly whisked
2 tablespoons unsalted butter, melted, at room temperature
2½ cups all-purpose flour, plus extra for dusting
Vegetable, canola, or rice bran oil, for deep-frying

FOR DUSTING
¼ cup firmly packed brown sugar
2 teaspoons ground cinnamon

RASPBERRY ICING
⅓ cup raspberries
1 cup confectioners' sugar

WHISK the 2 tablespoons of lukewarm water with the yeast in a small bowl. Add the sugar and whisk until well combined. Allow to stand in a warm spot for 10–15 minutes, or until frothy.

ADD the salt, cinnamon, vanilla extract, egg, butter, flour, the remaining ½ cup of water, and the yeast mixture to the bowl of a stand mixer. Attach the dough hook and mix together on medium speed until well combined, then mix for 5 minutes more, or until the dough is smooth and elastic (the dough will feel slightly sticky).

USING very lightly floured hands, scrape the dough into a lightly oiled bowl. Cover with a piece of parchment paper, then a dish towel and set aside to rest in a warm, draft-free spot for 1–1½ hours, or until the dough has doubled in size.

LIGHTLY flour a clean surface and rolling pin and roll the dough into a rectangle about 17 x 12 inches. Combine the brown sugar and cinnamon for dusting, then sprinkle it evenly over the surface of the dough. Roll the dough up tightly from the long side to form one long log. Trim the ends so that the log is about 16 inches in length.

LINE two baking trays with parchment paper. Cut the log into 12 equal pieces, then transfer to the lined baking trays, cut-side facing up. Lightly flatten each piece of dough with the palm of your hand to a ⅔ inch thick round. Cover the trays with dish towels and allow to rest for 1 hour at room temperature in a warm spot or until doubled in size.

HEAT the oil in a deep, heavy-based saucepan over medium–high heat until it reaches 350°F. Deep-fry the donuts in batches, turning occasionally, for 2–3 minutes each, or until puffed, golden, and cooked through. Transfer to paper towels to drain briefly, then transfer to a wire rack set over a baking tray.

MASH the raspberries for the icing with a fork in a small bowl, then push them through a fine sieve and discard any seeds left behind. Whisk the raspberry purée and confectioners' sugar together until well combined and smooth.

DRIZZLE the raspberry icing over the warm donuts, then allow to set before serving.

Donut tower cake

Halloween donuts

Strawberry heart donuts

Neapolitan ice-cream donut sandwiches

Champagne-cream donut bites

Christmas donuts

Chocolate sparkle donuts

CHAPTER 7

SHOW-STOPPERS AND JAW-DROPPERS

DONUT TOWER CAKE

This is the perfect celebratory cake for all ages, and will really wow your guests. Get everyone involved in the decorating to make it truly unique.

CAKE DONUTS

5 tablespoons + 2 teaspoons unsalted butter, at room temperature
½ cup superfine sugar
1 egg, at room temperature
1 egg yolk, at room temperature
1 teaspoon vanilla extract
1 cup milk
½ cup cocoa powder
4 cups self-rising flour, plus extra for dusting
A good pinch of fine sea salt
Vegetable, canola, or rice bran oil, for deep-frying

TO DECORATE

½ cup superfine sugar
Nonpareils and white sprinkles

RASPBERRY CREAM CHEESE ICING

2¾ tablespoons unsalted butter, at room temperature
4 oz package cream cheese, at room temperature
⅓ cup raspberries
1⅓ cups confectioners' sugar, plus extra for dusting

CREAM the butter and sugar together in the bowl of a stand mixer for 3 minutes, or until pale and fluffy. Add the egg, egg yolk, vanilla extract, and milk and mix until just combined.

SIFT the cocoa, flour and salt over the mixture in the bowl. Mix until just combined, but do not overmix or the dough will become tough.

LIGHTLY flour a clean surface, turn the dough out onto it and, using lightly floured hands, gently bring it together. Knead gently for a few seconds until the dough becomes smooth. Using a floured rolling pin, gently roll the dough out to a ⅓ inch thickness. Using a floured 3½ inch round cookie cutter, cut out rounds from the dough, making sure you cut them as close together as possible. Re-roll any scraps and cut out more rounds until you have 12 in total. Use a floured 1⅛ inch round cookie cutter to cut out holes from the center of each larger circle.

PUT the sugar for coating in a deep, heatproof bowl.

HEAT the oil in a deep, heavy-based saucepan over medium–high heat until it reaches 350°F. Deep-fry the donuts in batches, turning occasionally, for 2–3 minutes each, or until puffed, golden, and cooked through. Transfer to paper towels to drain briefly then, while still hot, roll only the edges of the donuts in sugar. Allow to cool.

BEAT the butter for the icing for 3 minutes, or until pale and creamy. Add the remaining icing ingredients and beat until well combined and smooth.

SPOON the icing over the tops of the cooled donuts. Stack the donuts in a tower on a cake stand. Decorate with the nonpareils and white sprinkles, then dust with extra confectioners' sugar before serving.

HALLOWEEN DONUTS

Impress your trick-or-treaters with these deliciously spooky pumpkin-pie donuts.

CAKE DONUTS

5 tablespoons + 2 teaspoons
  unsalted butter, at room
  temperature
½ cup superfine sugar
1 egg, at room temperature
1 egg yolk, at room temperature
1 teaspoon vanilla extract
½ teaspoon pumpkin pie spice
¾ cup cooked and mashed
  pumpkin
⅓ cup milk
4⅓ cups self-rising flour,
  plus extra for dusting
A good pinch of fine sea salt
Vegetable, canola, or rice bran
  oil, for deep-frying

VANILLA NUTMEG GLAZE

1½ cups confectioners' sugar
2 teaspoons vanilla bean paste
A good pinch of freshly
  grated nutmeg

TO SERVE

1½ cups caramel popcorn,
  broken into pieces
Black writing gel

CREAM the butter and sugar together in the bowl of a stand mixer for 3 minutes, or until pale and fluffy. Add the egg, egg yolk, vanilla extract, pumpkin pie spice, pumpkin, and milk and mix until just combined.

SIFT the flour and salt over the mixture in the bowl. Mix until just combined, but do not overmix or the dough will become tough.

LIGHTLY flour a clean surface, turn the dough out onto it and, using lightly floured hands, gently bring it together. Knead gently for a few seconds until the dough becomes smooth. Using a floured rolling pin, gently roll the dough out to a ⅓ inch thickness. Using a floured 3½ inch round cookie cutter, cut out rounds from the dough, making sure you cut them as close together as possible. Re-roll any scraps and cut out more rounds until you have 12 in total. Use a floured 1⅛ inch round cookie cutter to cut out holes from the center of each larger circle.

HEAT the oil in a deep, heavy-based saucepan over medium–high heat until it reaches 350°F. Deep-fry the donuts in batches for 2–3 minutes each, turning occasionally, or until puffed, golden, and cooked through. Transfer to paper towels to drain briefly, then allow to cool.

WHISK all the ingredients for the glaze together in a bowl with 2 tablespoons of water until well combined and smooth.

DIP the cooled donuts, one at a time, into the glaze. Transfer to a wire rack set over a baking tray. Sprinkle the tops with caramel popcorn, then decorate with black writing gel and allow to set before serving.

STRAWBERRY HEART DONUTS

Spoil your true love with these little bites of strawberry sweetness. So much better than a bunch of roses.

CAKE DONUTS

5 tablespoons + 2 teaspoons unsalted butter, at room temperature
½ cup superfine sugar
1 egg, at room temperature
1 egg yolk, at room temperature
1 teaspoon vanilla extract
¾ cup milk
4 cups self-rising flour, plus extra for dusting
A good pinch of fine sea salt
1½ cups freeze-dried strawberries
Vegetable, canola, or rice bran oil, for deep-frying

STRAWBERRY ICING

1 cup confectioners' sugar, plus extra for dusting
2 teaspoons imitation strawberry extract
1 tablespoon milk
6 drops of pink food coloring

CREAM the butter and sugar together in the bowl of a stand mixer for 3 minutes, or until pale and fluffy. Add the egg, egg yolk, vanilla extract, and milk and mix until just combined.

SIFT the flour and salt over the mixture in the bowl. Add half of the freeze-dried strawberries and mix until just combined, but do not overmix or the dough will become tough.

LIGHTLY flour a clean surface, turn the dough out onto it and, using lightly floured hands, gently bring it together. Knead gently for a few seconds until the dough becomes smooth. Using a floured rolling pin, gently roll the dough out to a ⅓ inch thickness. Using a floured 2⅓ inch heart-shaped cookie cutter, cut out hearts from the dough, making sure you cut them as close together as possible. Re-roll any scraps and cut out more hearts until you have 18 in total.

HEAT the oil in a deep, heavy-based saucepan over medium–high heat until it reaches 350°F. Deep-fry the donuts in batches, turning occasionally, for 2–3 minutes each, or until puffed, golden, and cooked through. Transfer to paper towels to drain briefly, then allow to cool.

WHISK all the ingredients for the strawberry icing together in a bowl until well combined and smooth.

TRANSFER the donuts to a wire rack set over a baking tray. Drizzle the icing over the cooled donuts. Sprinkle the tops with the remaining freeze-dried strawberries, then allow to set before dusting with extra confectioners' sugar and serving.

NEAPOLITAN ICE-CREAM DONUT SANDWICHES

A great summer outdoor treat.

CAKE DONUTS
5 tablespoons + 2 teaspoons
    unsalted butter, at room
    temperature
½ cup superfine sugar
1 egg, at room temperature
1 egg yolk, at room temperature
1 teaspoon vanilla extract
¾ cup milk
4 cups self-rising flour,
    plus extra for dusting
A good pinch of fine sea salt
Vegetable, canola, or rice bran
    oil, for deep-frying

VANILLA ICING
1 cup confectioners' sugar
1 teaspoon vanilla extract
1 tablespoon boiling water

STRAWBERRY ICING
1 cup confectioners' sugar
1 teaspoon imitation
    strawberry extract
8 drops of red food coloring
1 tablespoon boiling water

CHOCOLATE ICING
⅔ cup confectioners' sugar
2 tablespoons cocoa powder
2 tablespoons boiling water

TO SERVE
Nonpareils
12 scoops Neapolitan ice cream

CREAM the butter and sugar together in the bowl of a stand mixer for 3 minutes, or until pale and fluffy. Add the egg, egg yolk, vanilla extract, and milk and mix until just combined.

SIFT the flour and salt over the mixture in the bowl. Mix until just combined, but do not overmix or the dough will become tough.

LIGHTLY flour a clean surface, turn the dough out onto it and, using lightly floured hands, gently bring it together. Knead gently for a few seconds until the dough becomes smooth. Using a floured rolling pin, gently roll the dough out to a ⅓ inch thickness. Using a floured 3½ inch round cookie cutter, cut out rounds from the dough, making sure you cut them as close together as possible. Re-roll any scraps and cut out more rounds until you have 12 in total.

HEAT the oil in a deep, heavy-based saucepan over medium–high heat until it reaches 350°F. Deep-fry the donuts in batches, turning occasionally, for 2–3 minutes each, or until puffed, golden, and cooked through. Transfer to paper towels to drain briefly, then allow to cool completely.

WHISK together the ingredients for each icing in separate bowls until well combined and smooth.

SPOON the icing over the donuts so you have four iced with vanilla, four with strawberry, and four with chocolate. Transfer the donuts to a wire rack set over a baking tray and sprinkle their tops with nonpareils. Allow to set.

WHEN you're ready to serve, carefully cut each donut in half and place a scoop of ice cream at the center. Replace the top and serve immediately.

CHAMPAGNE-CREAM DONUT BITES

These exquisite bites will make any celebration extra special.

YEAST DONUTS

¼ cup lukewarm water
3½ teaspoons dried yeast
3⅔ cups all-purpose flour,
    plus extra for dusting
¼ cup superfine sugar
½ teaspoon fine sea salt
1 egg, at room temperature,
    lightly whisked
2½ tablespoons unsalted butter,
    melted, at room temperature
¾ cup Champagne
Vegetable, canola, or rice bran
    oil, for deep-frying
1⅔ cups crème anglaise
    or vanilla pudding

TO COAT

1 cup sugar
2 teaspoons edible sliver glitter,
    plus extra, to serve

ROYAL ICING

1 egg white, at room temperature
1½ cups confectioners' sugar
1 teaspoon lemon juice

WHISK the water and yeast together in a small bowl. Add 1 teaspoon of the flour and 1 teaspoon of the sugar and whisk until well combined. Leave at room temperature in a warm spot f or 10–15 minutes, or until frothy.

PLACE the remaining flour, remaining sugar, and the salt in the bowl of a stand mixer. Attach the dough hook and mix together on medium speed until well combined.

WITH the motor running, slowly add the egg, melted butter, champagne, and then the yeast mixture. Mix for 8 minutes, or until the dough is smooth and elastic (the dough should feel slightly sticky).

USING very lightly floured hands, scrape the dough into a lightly oiled bowl. Cover with a piece of parchment paper, then a dish towel. Set aside to rest at room temperature in a warm, draft-free spot for 1–1½ hours, or until the dough has doubled in size.

LINE two large baking trays with parchment paper. Generously flour a work surface and gently tip the dough out onto it. Using a floured rolling pin, gently roll the dough out to a ⅓ inch thickness. Using a floured 2⅓ inch round cookie cutter, cut out 18 rounds from the dough, making sure you cut them as close together as possible. Carefully transfer the donuts to the prepared trays, spreading them out in a single layer. Cover with dish towels and let rest for 40 minutes at room temperature or until doubled in size.

COMBINE the sugar and edible silver glitter in a deep, heatproof bowl.

HEAT the oil in a deep, heavy-based saucepan over medium–high heat until it reaches 350°F. Deep-fry the donuts in batches, turning occasionally, for 2–3 minutes each, or until puffed, golden, and cooked through. Transfer to paper towels to drain briefly then, while still hot, toss in the silver glitter to coat. Allow to cool.

SPOON the crème anglaise or vanilla pudding into a piping bag fitted with a ¼ inch round tip. Pipe this into the donut centers.

BEAT the egg white for the royal icing until frothy, then add the confectioners' sugar, a tablespoon at a time, beating until the mixture is thick and glossy. Beat in the juice until combined. Spoon the icing into a piping bag fitted with a ⅓ inch round tip and pipe a small round on top of each donut. Sprinkle with the extra silver glitter and serve.

CHRISTMAS DONUTS

Not only do these donuts look the part, but every bite is full of traditional Christmas flavor.

CAKE DONUTS

5 tablespoons + 2 teaspoons unsalted butter, at room temperature
½ cup superfine sugar
1 egg, at room temperature
1 egg yolk, at room temperature
1 teaspoon vanilla extract
¾ cup milk
¾ cup mincemeat (vegetarian)
4⅓ cups self-rising flour, plus extra for dusting
A good pinch of fine sea salt
Vegetable, canola, or rice bran oil, for deep-frying

TO COAT

1 cup sugar
2 teaspoons ground cinnamon

BRANDY ICING

1 cup confectioners' sugar
2 teaspoons imitation brandy extract
3 teaspoons boiling water

TO SERVE

Red and green sprinkles

CREAM the butter and sugar together in the bowl of a stand mixer for 3 minutes, or until pale and fluffy. Add the egg, egg yolk, vanilla extract, milk, and mincemeat and mix until just combined.

SIFT the flour and salt over the mixture in the bowl. Mix until just combined, but do not overmix or the dough will become tough.

LIGHTLY flour a clean surface, turn the dough out onto it and, using lightly floured hands, gently bring it together. Knead gently for a few seconds until the dough becomes smooth. Using a floured rolling pin, gently roll the dough out to a ⅓ inch thickness. Using a floured 3½ inch round cookie cutter, cut out rounds from the dough, making sure you cut them as close together as possible. Re-roll any scraps and cut out more rounds until you have 12 in total. Use a floured 1⅛ inch round cookie cutter to cut out holes from the center of each larger circle.

COMBINE the sugar and cinnamon, for coating the donuts, in a deep, heatproof bowl.

HEAT the oil in a deep, heavy-based saucepan over medium–high heat until it reaches 350°F. Deep-fry the donuts in batches, turning occasionally, for 2–3 minutes each, or until puffed, golden, and cooked through. Transfer to paper towels to drain briefly then, while still hot, roll in the cinnamon sugar to coat on all sides. Allow to cool.

WHISK all the ingredients for the brandy icing together until well combined and smooth.

DRIZZLE the icing over the donuts. Transfer to a wire rack set over a baking tray, then top with the sprinkles. Allow to set before serving.

CHOCOLATE SPARKLE DONUTS

Give any special occasion all the glitz and glamour it deserves with these stand-out treats, using touches of edible gold to keep the night sparkly.

YEAST DONUTS
1 cup lukewarm milk
3½ teaspoons dried yeast
3⅔ cups all-purpose flour,
    plus extra for dusting
¼ cup superfine sugar
½ teaspoon fine sea salt
1 egg, at room temperature,
    lightly whisked
2 tablespoons unsalted butter,
    melted, at room temperature
Vegetable, canola, or rice bran
    oil, for deep-frying

CHOCOLATE GANACHE
7 oz (7 squares) dark chocolate,
    chopped
¼ cup light cream

TO SERVE
1½ cups chocolate pudding
Edible gold glitter, mini stars
    and gold dragees

WHISK the milk and yeast together in a small bowl. Add 1 teaspoon of the flour and 1 teaspoon of the sugar and whisk until well combined. Allow to stand at room temperature in a warm spot for 10–15 minutes or until frothy.

PLACE the remaining flour, remaining sugar, and the salt in the bowl of a stand mixer. Attach the dough hook and mix together on medium speed until well combined.

WITH the motor running, slowly add the egg, melted butter, and the yeast mixture. Mix for 8 minutes, or until the dough is smooth and elastic (the dough should feel slightly sticky).

USING very lightly floured hands, scrape the dough into a lightly oiled bowl. Cover with a piece of parchment paper, then a dish towel. Set aside to rest at room temperature in a warm, draft-free spot for 1–1½ hours, or until the dough has doubled in size.

LINE two large baking trays with parchment paper. Generously flour a work surface and gently tip the dough out onto it. Using a floured rolling pin, gently roll the dough out to a ⅓ inch thickness. Using a floured 3½ inch round cookie cutter, cut out 10 rounds from the dough, making sure you cut them as close together as possible. Use a floured 1⅛ inch round cookie cutter to cut out holes from the center of each larger circle. Carefully transfer to the prepared trays, spreading them out in a single layer. Cover with dish towels and rest for 40 minutes at room temperature or until doubled in size.

HEAT the oil in a deep, heavy-based saucepan over medium–high heat until it reaches 350°F. Deep-fry the donuts in batches, turning occasionally, for 2–3 minutes each, or until puffed, golden, and cooked through. Transfer to paper towels to drain. Cool, then cut in half.

PLACE all the ingredients for the chocolate ganache in a heatproof bowl set over a simmering saucepan of water, making sure the base of the bowl doesn't touch the water. Stir gently until the mixture melts and is smooth. Remove the bowl from the heat, and cool to room temperature, stirring occasionally, for 1 hour, or until set softly to a spreadable consistency.

SPOON the chocolate pudding over one cut-side of each donut, then replace the donut tops. Spread the tops with ganache, then sprinkle with gold glitter, stars, and dragees and serve.

Index

Page numbers in italics refer to photographs.

STERLING EPICURE
New York

An Imprint of Sterling Publishing
1166 Avenue of the Americas
New York, NY 10036

STERLING EPICURE is a trademark of Sterling Publishing Co., Inc.
The distinctive Sterling logo is a registered trademark of Sterling Publishing Co., Inc.

This Sterling Epicure edition published in 2015
First published in 2014 by Murdoch Books, an imprint of Allen & Unwin

Publisher: Jane Morrow
Editorial Manager: Virginia Birch
Design Manager: Hugh Ford
Recipe Developer and Home Economist: Tracey Meharg
Editor: Katie Bosher
Design: Dan Peterson & Jacqui Porter, Northwood Green
Photographer: Rob Palmer
Stylist: Michelle Noerianto
Assistant Home Economist: Theressa Klein
Production Manager: Mary Bjelobrk

Text © Murdoch Books 2014
The moral rights of the author have been asserted.
Design © Murdoch Books 2014
Photography © Murdoch Books 2014

All rights reserved. No part of this publication may be reproduced, stored in a retrieval system,
or transmitted in any form or by any means (including electronic, mechanical, photocopying,
recording, or otherwise) without prior written permission from the publisher.

ISBN 978-1-4549-1775-5

Distributed in Canada by Sterling Publishing
c/o Canadian Manda Group, 664 Annette Street
Toronto, Ontario, Canada M6S 2C8

For information about custom editions, special sales, and premium and corporate purchases,
please contact Sterling Special Sales at 800-805-5489 or specialsales@sterlingpublishing.com.

Manufactured in China

2 4 6 8 10 9 7 5 3 1

www.sterlingpublishing.com

IMPORTANT: Those who might be at risk from the effects of salmonella poisoning (the elderly,
pregnant women, young children, and those suffering from immune deficiency diseases) should
consult their doctor with any concerns about eating raw egg.